MW01492681

THE PRESSURE OF PAIN

ADDIE M. GRIFFIN

CANDACE JOYNER
PUBLISHING

Copyright © 2021 by Addie M. Griffin

All rights reserved. No part of this publication may be reproduced by any means, graphics, electronic, or mechanical, including photocopying, recording, taping, or by any information storage retrieval system without the written permission of the publisher except in the case of brief quotations embodied in critical articles and reviews.

Candace Joyner Publishing
PO Box 310
Lumberton, NC 28359
www.candacejoyner.com
candacejoyner2020@gmail.com

Unless otherwise indicated, scripture is taken from the King James Version. Scripture quotations marked (NIV) are taken from the Holy Bible, New International Version®, NIV®. Copyright © 1973, 1978, 1984,2011 by Biblica, Inc.™

Used by permission of Zondervan. All rights reserved worldwide. www.zondervan.com The "NIV" and "New International Version" are trademarks registered in the United States Patent and Trademark Office by Biblica, Inc.™ Scripture quotations marked (NKJV) are taken from the New King James Version®. Copyright © 1982 by Thomas Nelson. Used by permission. All rights reserved.

"Scripture quotations taken from the Amplified® Bible (AMP), Copyright © 2015 by The Lockman Foundation used by permission. www.Lockman.org"

The Pressure of Pain/Addie M. Griffin

ISBN- 978-1-7355284-6-5

Disclaimer:

This book contains 100% facts, and can be proven, according to my memories and recollection of my experiences and things that took place in my life. Many of the living's names, unlike the deceased have been changed, to protect privacy. Most places I recall as where I've lived, and in surrounding Akron, Ohio, are true and accurate.

Finally, I cannot, and will not apologize for my truth.

Table of Contents

Acknowledgements

First and foremost, I'm not just thanking God (Yahweh), I'm giving Him all the glory, and telling you that without Him, none of this would be possible.

Secondly, to my children, all six of you all are strong, endured my pain and much of my struggle and decided to love me anyways, I want to thank you and dedicate this book to you.

Special thanks to Kendra Sikes, you helped me write my truth and wouldn't let me quit even when I wanted to, and to my publisher Candace Joyner; Prophetess you gave me the push I needed to birth this book, to both of you, I say thank you.

Lastly, but definitely not the least, I want to appreciate my Daddy Raymond L. Griffin whom I dedicate this book to. I miss you so much dad. I always wanted to make you proud. I love you and can't wait to see you again.

Dedication

This book is dedicated to my beloved daughter Jessica Lynn Griffin born December 4, 1990, and who died January 17, 2021, at the age of 30 from COVID-19, While I was still getting this book together. I always wanted to make you proud of me, and happy to be my daughter, and me your mother. May you smile from heaven upon me your brother's and sister's and all your friends and loved ones. There will never be another Jessica, loved by so many.

Words cannot express how deeply you will be missed! How deeply I loved you. How hard it has been to move on without you. My only comfort is knowing we were moving towards building our relationship months before the day you died. Forever you are in my heart, my firstborn child. I will never forget your smile and laugh, and I can't wait until I see you again, my beautiful child.

Dedications to the Griffin family

To those who have fallen asleep, awaiting the return of our LORD
Jesus Christ and to those of us still living, I dedicate this book to
you and enter it as a part of our legacy.

Note to my readers

Writing this book was truly a journey of reliving my past. At times it was hard; so hard I quit and gave up a few times. My desire to move on was inspired by you; what I could give to you, as well as my desire to impact the world with something real; my transparency and something positive for the reader to think upon. Above all, my desire to move on with the book was inspired by my longing to transform lives, through Christ Jesus who lives in me.

If you can identify with me in the things, I went through in my story; great, but please don't glory in it! It's a part of my past, and that is all it will ever be! Focus on my forward movement and the freedom through Christ which I received. Focus on how big and great our God is and that through Him, and only Him can we receive mercy, grace, forgiveness and freedom!!!

Finally, I received a lot of healing through writing this book. I want to inspire and encourage you to do the same! Remember, it is the job of the enemy to remind you of your past and to keep you there. God says when we ask for forgiveness, He remembers no more! Deal with your past, ask forgiveness from God for the things you have done, and forgive yourself! Don't continue to relive it!

Be encouraged,

With love,

Addie.

Introduction

We all can agree right now that everyone has experienced pain at one point or the other in their lives. No one on this earth can escape pain. Pain is categorized as a general feeling of suffering and discomfort. There are many ways for us to 'cover and mask' the pain, 'carry' the pain, and 'release' the pain. That pain is the very thing that we dare not speak of because it will expose whom we really are. Vessels filled with pain, carrying it around, and trying hard to cover and mask it, and carry it when we need to release it positively.

The title of this book, "The Pressure of Pain" was impressed upon me so heavily by God when I read a study on The Pressures of the man Job. Job practically lost everything ...E V E R Y T H I N G! Not just his material possessions but his children, his cattle, his home and his wife too. Job's wife even told him to give up on the most important person in his life, which is God; everything near and dear to Job, was gone. This book is being written irst to expose the pain I experienced. We release the pain so we can learn from it and be healed, and also for others who have experienced similar things. There are many ways to carry pain. Ask the 24.6 million Americans who are addicted to drugs; choosing to carry the pain negatively, or the many Americans in incarceration who chose to release their pain negatively. Pain will force something to happen, from its persuasive and influential nature. Pressure will also cause something to happen, but when doubled with pain, it can cause you to move towards finding a solution to fix and correct the pain. While you wait for that answer, you will have plenty of solutions to try. Things that will reduce the pain, temporarily band-aides which we often use to mask, cover-up or nurse the pain. Till date, man has exhausted every device in this sinful world to provide pleasure, to feed an ego, to feed pride, and everything else contrary to God. We must look to God to fix our pain and provide a solution for us, in order to make us better; instead of hurting us. Many of us run from God and choose to blame Him for our pain. The truth in Job's case is that it was allowed as a test to him. Many of us have caused our own pain and mishaps, and many of us have had the calls of God over our lives which were essential to the crushing of pain circumstances and even things we couldn't control. Either way, the solution is still God, He is the only One who can fix and heal and give us the right solutions to relieve our pain.

This book is about the pain that I went through in my life, and how the more I ran away, the hurt and pain, kept bringing me back to God, how I found God, how He turned every bad thing in my life into good; just as the scripture in Romans 8:28 states. Even though the pain endured, I learned how to function, tolerate and grow in that same pain, and as well count it all joy as I allowed Him to be my strength in my weakness. I used the very same pain as a steppingstone to a better me in God, and He was there in every step of the way. Enough pressure will cause a breakthrough, and if you let Him handle your pain, He will carry it as you give it to Him. This is my personal journey through pain, forgiveness, healing, and restoration, and for that, I give all glory to Him. Pain (trials) produces something so much greater within us, than the pain itself spiritual endurance, and greater faith, patience. Let God change you and the outcome of your pain, as He did for me!

James 1:2-4 (Amplified); Consider it nothing but joy, my brothers and sisters, whenever you fall into various trials. Be assured that the testing of your faith [through experience] produces endurance [leading to spiritual maturity, and inner peace]. And let endurance have its perfect result and do a thorough work, so that you may be perfect and completely developed [in your faith], lacking in nothing.

_____

_____

_____

_____

_____

_____

Pray this prayer:

Heavenly Father, ...As I read this book, turn my pressure and pain into power, and allow it to change me. Allow forgiveness to flood my heart and allow me to make a choice to use this pain for my benefit, and then release it to You! Help me to open my heart and mind to receive from You. Allow me to heal from my past, and to move forward to help others, all by your own power and grace.

... in Jesus' mighty name, Amen!

Prologue
"The Foundation of My Pain"

I was born in Akron, Ohio, a small city south of Cleveland. Ohio home to about 197,633 people. To the outside world those who have never lived here, it seems like a small, unrecognized, little hick town. To me, this is rather a home. I knew everybody, and everybody knew me. I had no shortage of friends to play with, or fun things to get into on a day-to-day basis; life was good. The older people in my neighborhood were just like parents to me. While growing up, the popular saying, "it takes a village to raise a child" was actually at work.

I was born at St. Thomas hospital, one of three major hospitals in Akron, Ohio. This was a non-denominational non-profit general hospital that opened in 1922 and was originally operated by the Sisters of Charity of St. Augustine. Then on August 16, 1935, one of the founders of Alcoholics Anonymous, admitted the first alcoholic patient with acute gastritis. This incident would make St. Thomas Hospital, the first in the world to treat alcoholism as a medical condition. Many years later, this same hospital closed the doors to its emergency room for good and became a full service psychiatric and orthopedic hospital.

Born on May 31, 1975, which was Memorial Day that year, I was the first child born to Brenda and Raymond Griffin. They married roughly two months before I was born on March 7th, and my mother was seven months pregnant with me at the time. She told me when I got older that they had just a court-house wedding. It was my mom's first marriage, but my dad's second one. I would find out later that I wasn't his first child either. I had a brother, who was two years older than me; that, my dad claimed. I never got to meet my brother until I was about eight, my brother came and stayed the whole summer with us, during the year I turned 8. I remember he reminded me of Daddy in looks, and he was tall. I was excited to have a brother!

My dad was 6'3; Carmel-complected with curly dark hair and a successful businessman. He worked at IBM computers and taught at local high schools. Eventually he opened his own real estate business. My mom was currently in nursing school, pursuing her RN degree while being a full-time mom. I remember the countless times I would see her studying and reading and preparing for tests. They both were pursuing "The American Dream." My mom could draw paint and do pictures of the Sesame Street characters in her spare time, and I remember her reading to me a lot. In 1977, my only sister Andrea, a 10-pound baby girl was born. My mom thought she was having a boy, but due to complications during her delivery of her lastborn child, she received a hysterectomy and could never again give birth to a son for my father. Mom even talked about the boy's name she had picked and expressed her love for the name, 'Jonathan.'

I remember bits and pieces of my childhood. Most of the tragedies I remember is from a little older age, but with no specific details. They say, 'scents can bring up emotions and thoughts from the past,' though I never cared to pursue that. One of my earliest memories is from age four, and since I was already reading by that time, my parents got me into a private school named Chapel Hill Christian School. I remember getting tested while in first grade and scoring at a 6th-grade reading level. That was a big deal back then to my parents; they couldn't stop talking about it. I learned at a young age to lose myself in a book because I loved to read. I believe that's what urged my parents to invest heavily in my education, and also send me to a private school. Often, I would finish my work ahead of the class because it wasn't challenging enough, and I would get bored. I would look for anyone to talk to, actually anyone who would listen. Being able to read as well as I did unlock so much potential in me. My dad always said I would make a great lawyer because I was good at debating things well and that he expected me to strive for the sky. I was extremely smart and strong willed at a very young age. I often expressed myself and as well had very strong likes and dislikes. At 5 years-old, he was constantly reminding me to keep my mind focused on my books and not on boys. This was a constant lecture, way before I ever even thought about a boy. He was my greatest support and would often listen to my ramblings but would impute me with knowledge daily.

Addie Marie was the name I was given. I was named after my dad's grandmother my great-grandmother. Growing up in the '80s, I didn't like my name; none of my schoolmates or anybody I knew had that name. In school. I chose to be called by my middle name Marie, but now that I'm older, Addie and Abby have become popular names. I prefer to be called Addie now due to the uniqueness of the name, and my nickname is Dee, short for Addie. Very rarely did I ever introduce myself as Addie, except at school or during business would they eventually find out my real name. Now that I am older, I have learned to appreciate the honor of being blessed with such a powerful name, and to be named after such a great person, loved by my dad. Whatever the case may be, my Daddy gave me this name, and I love it. My mom Brenda, was the youngest of four siblings, having two older brothers, and one older sister. They all grew up in Cambridge, Ohio, a city close to Columbus and Zanesville, Ohio. She had a stepdad who had been raising her since she was a little girl. The few times I met him, I thought he was her real dad and never had a reason to question it. From the earliest memory I had, he was the only maternal grandfather I knew. My mom looked a lot like my grandmother Jessie. She was pretty, with long black hair, 5'2 short, dark complected and very attractive. My mom separated from my dad a few times when we were young, mostly temporarily, and her parents took us in then.

We stayed at their family house for about a week or so. As I got older, I never developed a connection to my grandparents; never even remembered past my youth. My mom, when I got older would tell me stories about her past and how she grew up. She often told me how her parents would drink alcohol every weekend until they would start arguing and beating each other up. Next, they would go to church like everything was okay. My grandparents never went, but they sent their kids. My mom said she was depressed as a kid and never felt loved by her mother. She was often ridiculed and put down as she was the youngest. Church was a positive outlet for her as it built her faith in God as a child, but also gave her something to hope in due to her shattered home life. My Aunt Renee and my dad also attended the church that my mom was going to as a child. My aunt Renee would say often that my mom would ask about my dad because she thought he was cute and had a crush on him. My mom was thirteen, and my dad was fifteen, but they didn't get together back then. My dad was my mom's childhood crush. Years later, their paths ran into each other again at eighteen, however, my dad was drafted into the Vietnam War in 1969, six years before my birth.

In researching and looking for information about my mother's past, I needed to ask questions from people who knew me back then in order to try and understand my childhood a little better. What I found out blew my mind; I stumbled on some things I never knew about my past. It was true that my mother had her own dark past and hard childhood, a victim of emotional and sexual abuse by the hands of her stepdad. What I didn't know was that my dad was also emotionally abusing her. My mom felt the need to "protect" my sister from him and them (his family). He started spending time with me, so exclusively was more about ownership and me being "his" than anything. He made me and himself outsiders, due to his insecurities over my mom's cheating. My mom was a church girl, and she followed the Apostolic church teaching to the letter, no make-up, no pants, and no jewelry. My dad was her first and only partner.

I have never in my life heard her curse, seen her smoke a cigarette, drink alcohol, or use drugs. Now keep in mind; from the outside looking in, when I grew up, I thought this was perfection. She would keep us in church, and I was in church from as young as I could remember. I loved going to Sunday School. Mom would dress Andrea and I so cute. I remember those shiny patent leather shoes, and those little bobby socks, that fold down with lace around them. Saturday night was hair day, the day to get our hair done by mom. She would do ponytails and pretty barrettes, and knockers. As I went to church, my understanding opened, and I started wondering whom God was. I imagined Him being big and deep in the clouds and just out of reach.

My mother was diagnosed with bipolar depression in her early 20's. She told me that getting married and having children was the solution to her pain. She thought that by doing those things she would obtain her happiness again, but it made it worse still. Her husband, my daddy was a cheater and supposedly had a diagnosis of schizophrenia, from the war, which caused frequent mental episodes as well. My grandmother would swear that my mother was into witchcraft and that she had done something to her son, saying he was never like that before he met my mom. Of course, my grandmother didn't like my mother.

However, I do remember a certain lady from one of the churches we attended, who was older than our mother. Mom used to talk to her all the time, and always used to give her money. Sister Kent was her name, and Mom used to let her babysit us. I also remember that she often gave out psychic readings and I would guess the lottery numbers. She also specialized in helping people handle situations that were out of control, like a woman in a bad marriage such as my mother was. I tried not to get noticed as I wondered what this older woman was doing, in my heart I knew something wasn't right.

When we left Glenn St, my dad was in the middle of a "psychotic breakdown" and had dug a big hole in our back yard. He placed everything we owned in there, though I don't know when, but he snapped back from that point to the new house. We moved to Kenmore, into a very nice house on a street named Bigelow. I was so excited to move, I remember how huge the yard was, and I had my own room. Nevertheless, my life and the life of my family was about to drastically change. My dad was frequently gone when I would wake up, and I would be told that he got sick through the night. At 10-years-old, I had a lot of new things happening in my life. Everything that was my normal and my comfortable was about to change. Over time, all things I knew had become different. Everything, from my kindergarten years to my private time with my Daddy; it all slowed down and eventually ceased altogether. My Dad whom I still looked up to was a man who would frequently spank me (at least that's what they called it back then). Dad was often angry and not the man I knew and grew to love. Today it's called a beating, and it will cause C.S.B. [Children's Services Board] to become heavily involved in your home life situation. Their very purpose was to take children away from parents who abused, neglected or could not properly care for their children.

I was unusually smart, I read good and listened in on conversations I knew I shouldn't have. My mom kept explaining my dad was sick, but I couldn't tell. We didn't live at the new house for long. I would miss that house but not the school. I remember being in 3rd grade at Smith school. I was the only black girl in my class. It felt odd, I wasn't put down, I just felt out of place. By 3rd grade I had been switched between five different schools. I just wanted to be accepted and make friends.

The year was 1987 and that was the year that I would become familiar with C.S.B. Mom had just graduated from nursing school and was a Registered Nurse, who had a regular job working at Community Support Services with mental disabled patients. When we moved fulltime, my dad didn't live with us anymore. We would see him occasionally. It was told to us by our mother that he had mental issues and that we should steer clear of him when we see him or if he tries to contact us. He was unable to keep a job, he didn't look like himself, and he was completely different. Mom said he once threatened to kill her and us too, but I just wanted my dad back. I had never seen him act out like she said. I began to rebel against her for keeping me away from him. I remember waking up some morning, asking about Dad (after we moved to our new house) only to be told that he was in the hospital; my heart was gripped with fear. I didn't understand at all and couldn't stand to be without him. When I spoke to my mother about the confusion in my mind, she told me that he was sick in the mind, but not physically. She was speaking of mental illness, particularly Schizophrenia. She was basically telling me that my Daddy had an illness, with split personalities and the night before he had been saying weird things. For this reason, my mother had him picked up and committed to the hospital. Dad had served in the United States Army, very shortly, and they drafted him for the Vietnam War at the young age of 18. I heard my mom say that this is where his mental health issue originated from.

They diagnosed a lot of men from the Vietnam war period with PTSD [Post Traumatic Stress Disorder], due to the trauma and violence they witnessed. My father was a very professionally intelligent man, so much so that after he finished his time in the Army; he went to college and obtained a teaching degree. Eventually, he turned his attention to business and computers and started working at IBM computers in the late '80s. He went on to own his own real estate agency 'Full Circle Realty,' in West Akron. Despite my mother and father meeting at church, he ended up marrying someone else.

Nadine, my daddy's first wife was the exact opposite of my mother; from what I heard from my aunt and grandmother. She seemed like she was, from my child-like view. I just remember she was light-skinned, and I also heard that was my dad's preference. My mom was the total opposite; She was sheltered, naive, and very unworldly. It was said that Nadine had been sneaking around on my dad. My aunt Renee swore she went by their house and claimed a man was seen coming out of the house. When my aunt Renee went to the door, Nadine came to the door in a robe. I don't think they were married long, and they only had one son that is exactly two years older than me. My brother and Nadine moved back to her hometown of Michigan.

With my dad not at home, except myself, my mom and Andrea, I was unhappy. My dad, in whom I had this deep connection, went from family man to being absent; I longed for his attention and affections. With these so-called threats my dad supposedly made, we chose to constantly move, so he wouldn't know where we lived.

I remember seeing my father hit my mother once when I was around ten. We were at a tire shop on Arlington Street, and they were arguing. I looked out of the backseat window next to Andrea, and we saw our dad smack our mom. I didn't know what to think. They both got back in the car, and nobody said a word as he drove us home. I and Andrea looked at each other in disbelief; signaling to each other that we would talk about this later. Neither mom nor dad ever discussed this situation, and we neither heard them arguing that night.

I experienced depression because my life changed so drastically. I suddenly got so depressed one fateful day that I planned to make a jump off the cliff in our backyard. I told my mom this issue one day; after being questioned repeatedly about my whereabouts after school.

There were times I never came home, and she wanted answers as to why; why my grades were so bad, and why I had missed so many days from school. She would send me to school and drop me off at school, but quite frequently I never made it. I purposely hung out with outcast children; they didn't go to school either. I would wander over to their house to smoke, drink, have sex and chill during school hours with other kids and adults. Because of my many absences from school, this earned me a truancy reputation, and therefore the juvenile courts became involved. My mom told them all about my attempt to jump off the cliff, my bad attitude, and my unruly behaviors. This in turn earned me six months in a Residential Mental Hospital, and a diagnosis of Bipolar. I was being prescribed Lithium, a counselor, and a stay at Sagamore Hills Psychiatry Hospital for youth.

My mom visited a few times with Andrea vowing to be there for me. Outside my knowledge, she had filed for divorce from my dad. I wasn't happy about this when I found out. They were officially separated, but I couldn't do anything to change that. Their divorce had nothing to do with him being my daddy, I knew he loved me.

Out of the blue, after dealing with endless group sessions, listening to other kid's problems, my name was called over the loudspeaker; my heart dropped at that moment. As I walked up to the desk, I was beckoned to the conference room. I remembered this wasn't the normal visitation day. As soon as I saw him, I screamed loudly. Dad came around. A fresh haircut, beard trimmed, smelling good; I hugged his neck as I said hello. He talked about his new place, his desire to move me in with him, and the importance of me finishing school. I was so happy to see him, but I noticed something different about him. While we talked, he kept asking me whether I heard something. It seemed there was something or someone else in the room. I told him I didn't hear anything, but he looked around and kept talking. It worried me because a girl I was friends within this very hospital frequently did that, hearing voices. I think that was the very reason she was there, because she spoke out to someone. I kept that between us. I never really thought about it again.

After I got out, I found out that my dad was at my grandmother's house, basically every day; so, this daddy's girl would make her way to grandma's house every chance she could. Combining the frequent visits to my dad and my friends, I just felt like I could do whatever I wanted, so I fell back into my old ways. My mom, fed up with not knowing where I was, my missing school, her having to leave work, she became tired of my behavior. I was voluntarily given to C.S.B. at 11 years old; awarded to the state, because I was out of control, as my mother told them. and she could no longer take care of me anymore which meant I would become a ward of the state. With a plan to visit and work on reunification at some point, I was dropped off by my mother to this place of unwanted, hurt, and abused kids. I would fit right in that I was hurt, I was abandoned and neglected by my mom and dad.

It wasn't long before I found ways, people, and things, to fill the feeling of pain. I stayed to myself, but since I was so filled with anger, I was an 11-year-old walking time bomb, wanting somebody to push me, so I would have a reason to fight. Anger became an outlet for my pain; a shield I wore as it was easier for me to show then; my tears or my weakness. Anger was my companion. I kept my fist bald up. A mean comment or a dirty look was my cover. C.S.B. was literally like a campus equipped with dorms for the girls and a couple of dorms for the boys. A large recreation center that was equipped with a pool table, music and just a fun place where we could spend time together. Everyone in every dorm could mingle under the staff watch, of course. So those of us who indulged in activities that the staff would not approve of, such as smoking, drinking, and excessive boy contact went off into an area where nobody saw us.

Up on a hill, at Clark St. The East Side had a drive-through that sold alcohol and cigarettes, across the street. To get them, all you had to do was stand there for a minute and wait until you saw somebody cool, or one who looked cool and could pull it off. By this time, I had been in the C.S.B. for nearly a month, and already I had a boyfriend. His nickname was Sin. He was a 15-year-old, troubled young man. I think I was attracted to his pain more than anything else. He was emotional when he spoke about his past and why he was there. Although our stories were different, I felt his pain, and that's what we had in common. He wrote poetry, I never saw him angry, he was soft-spoken, but sad. He often spoke about death and suicide, but when he saw me, his eyes lit up, and he smiled, making me feel great every time I saw him. He had his boys with whom he ran with; Whiz (Robert Bowen), Chris Warren, and Kebo. I had my girls; Erica, Gretchen and Michel'le. My girls were older; I think I was one of the youngest girls there. I was almost 12; the little sister they dragged around because I was cute and kept my mouth shut. I loved hanging around these girls; they made me feel grown-up. Pretending to be older, nobody ever knew any of whom I really was, but Sin knew everything, and I kept it real with him, as he accepted me.

My dad came to visit me on a certain Wednesday in the spring, so we got to walk around on campus. He talked again about meeting with my caseworker Elaine Stephens, to get me out of there, and about having a new place on Packard Street, and getting a new job too. He also explained that he couldn't be with my mother anymore, but that he loved me and loved Andrea too. I thought back in my mind, I never saw them kiss, hug, or get affectionate ever. Hearing from my grandma and Aunt Renee, they acted like she never was someone he could ever desire. I heard that she never really had a relationship with her mother but was raised by her mother's mother, who was my great grandma. She never displayed affection towards me, unlike with Andrea. I was labeled a "Daddy's Girl" and eventually began to feel like an outsider. Was I being punished because I loved and wanted to spend time with my dad? This was the reason I never wanted to be there. She never took that special time with me, unlike with Andrea. My dad asked if I needed any money, and he did that right before he was about to leave the visit. I replied, "Yes" to him. Holding my hand out in anticipation, he went straight for his wallet. I thanked him, and we hugged each other and kissed, and said our goodbyes.

I walked away hopeful, feeling like he would soon rescue me and get me out of that place. I was currently awaiting placement in a group home, which was the plan of action if my dad didn't rescue me fast. Today as I walked away from him after the conversation we had, I believed he was going to come through for me, unlike my mom who thrived, on placing me in these types of places because she claimed she couldn't control me. I met up with Sin after my visit, I mentioned the five dollars, and before I knew it, we agreed to go to the drive-thru and spend it on some alcohol. Now, I had sipped beer before, but never have I been drunk ever, and never had even tasted liquor much less MD/20/20. Back in the day we would go to drive-thru and stores and wait to see someone cool who would cop/buy what we needed. I was a good judge of character and looked older for my age, it didn't work all the time and sometimes we had sat a while to ask the right person.

I, Sin, one of his boys, and one of my girls sat drinking and passing the bottle between ourselves. Then it happened; everything started spinning, and I lost control. I briefly remember doing cartwheels off the hill we were sitting on; flashes of Sin, and my girl telling me to chill out before the staff finds out. Feelings of wanting to throw up and lastly, lying in bed. I'm groggy at this point; I knew I was busted when I heard this staff lady say they were notifying my parents. I had a headache, my whole body ached, and I was in trouble, not only with these people but with my dad! Thursday, I woke up with a new perspective; I was on restriction, my privileges had been taken away, and my parents had been informed. I knew I would have to face the music, but my mom wasn't surprised to hear me do things like this; it's just how she viewed me.

I decided to call my dad instead and tell him the whole story. I found him at my grandma's house, and he wasn't mad; just a little disappointed. He let me know he loved me, and that all was well, and that I was forgiven. I was stuck in the Receiving Unit all weekend. I hadn't even moved to the girl's dorm yet, so my stay was uncertain. Sin came and visited me by lightly tapping on my window, knowing I was on restriction. We laughed and talked, even about the night I was drunk, and he told me all the crazy things I said and did, which I could not remember. Monday morning, we had a very hot day, but the clouds were dark and surfacing, so it was about to rain. Suddenly I heard my name over the loudspeaker, but as I contemplated the walk it was May 18, 1987, so I wonder what they wanted. Did the group at home finally have a bed, assuming my dad had come on the rescue mission? As I approached the main desk to identify whom I was, the receptionist beckoned me to take a seat. As I sat down, Elaine showed up. She led me to the conference room, but nothing could prepare me for what was to come. Inside the conference room was my mother who was crying beside her sister, Vivian, who was supporting her. I can't recall if they mentioned it or if I just felt I knew. I ran and ran and never looked back. My Dad had been found dead, in his car parked in front of my grandmother's house on the corner of

Roslyn and Copley Rd. As soon as I left that building, it began to rain; I get sad now when it rains, it reminds me of his death.

2nd Corinthians 1:3-4: "Praise be to the God and Father of Our Lord Jesus Christ, the God of compassion and the God of all comfort, who comforts us in all our troubles, so we can comfort those in any trouble with the comfort we ourselves receive from God." [NLT].

_____

_____

_____

_____

_____

_____

Pray this prayer along with me:

Heavenly Father, let us be aware of others pain, may we reach out in pure love, even to the extent of our enemies. Let us not walk away, but give us compassion for one another, make us make it our business to be there for one another, if not in person, always through prayer...

...in Jesus' mighty name, Amen!

Chapter 1
"The Entry of My Pain"

After my father died, I don't need to spell out the fact that my world came to an end, right? Essentially, that day I lost both of my parents; my mother for abandoning me, and my father in his death. My only steady support was my grandmother Ann, whose house I spent most of my days after his death. My father at 35-years-old had been found dead in his car with a gun (a 38 special in his lap), from a self-inflicted gunshot wound to the head. This information came from my Aunt Renee, who found him and was the last person to see him alive. She said she had an appointment and needed to take her newborn, who was 18 days old to the doctor, so she called her brother. She said that when he arrived; he was a bit impatient and informed her that he had something to do at 1 o'clock (an appointment of some sorts). He was rushing her to get ready, then said that he would meet her in the car, and he offered to take his nephew down with him, but she refused, saying "she would be down in a minute." So, imagine the look on my aunt's face when she came to get into the car, with my little cousin in her hands? To discover her brother dead, I could not even imagine. She mentioned that leading up to this, there were things she was really concerned about, and she even got to blame my mother for my father's death. My Aunt Renee mentioned that two weeks before his death that he was normal, until my mom called him over to the apartment, in order to discuss some things about me. She also mentioned that my dad once said my mother kept offering him a sandwich which he eventually accepted. She then said that after he came over, he was never the same after that.

My aunt also said that shortly later he left, he began to hear voices and to act weirdly around her; that's when it occurred to her. She really felt my mom was responsible for his death. Not that my mom was most popular amongst my dad's people, they never liked her, but when it came to his death, they hated and blamed her. Mom didn't even put a dime towards his funeral, and that added more fuel to the fire. Mom made sure she received death benefits and a widow's pension, and also collected survivors benefits for me and my sister. I don't think I spoke to her at the funeral, so mad I was and worse still that my dad was dead. Shortly after my dad's funeral, I had to report back to C.S.B. I hated that place, and now I felt vulnerable because I knew that everybody knew. The staff and other kids were apologizing and offering condolences, which made me even mad. I got mad one day and punched a staff member in the face.

At age twelve, going on thirteen I was heading to my first group home, Oesterlen Service for Youth in Springfield, Ohio. I wasn't happy at any place, and I wasn't about to follow anybody's rules, so I ran away a lot. I ran to feel free from myself, the hurt, and the pain, but with no destination. I became older and wiser and linked up with some girls that knew the streets. Although the place was not bad, they often took us swimming and horseback riding. I couldn't see any fun in that though. I wanted to be free, not contained, and to go by my own rules actually. I had a boyfriend whom I met in there, and Roland was his name, but nobody was actually significant, and no one truly got my attention. I had a lot of boys who liked me, even to grown men. I was cute and could get anybody I wanted, or so I thought. I began to be promiscuous with relationships. When I was due to leave

Oesterlen Service for Youth, I didn't think about anybody; not even the friends I met there.

I left there and was just waiting to go to the next place. Ironton, Ohio was the next group home, close to Kentucky and there was no running away from there. You know I actually tried to, right? The place wasn't that bad, they did have a lot of fun activities. I remember being there for Christmas, and we all had to produce a Christmas list. I wanted a Nintendo and a Mario game, which was exactly what I opened. Shortly after my 13th birthday, I graduated from group homes to a couple foster homes and to actual jail, D.Y.S. At 14. When it didn't work out in the group home setting, jail was the only other route they could go, and I was sent there for six months. I was locked up and for once couldn't run away. I spent my whole teen years in group homes, a few foster homes, and eventually juvenile jail until I was eighteen.

My mom would visit me, send money religiously, and make sure I always had what I needed. I guessed that was her way to express love. Being the best dressed and having money in my commissary made me look good to others. Inside, I was a lonely, hurt and angry, little girl who was actually a walking time bomb, warming up to explode. Instead of speaking my feelings, I expressed it in anger, in the rage, and the fighting. None of the many classes offered by the group homes or by the D.Y.S. could help me. I lacked love, and that was the real problem. I went on my own quest to find it, not sure what it looked like but needing that feeling. Like What I had seen on TV, like the honey nut cheerios commercial, showing kids dancing with their parents.

What I missed growing up as a child, a mother's love. An embrace, a kiss, a reassurance that she loved me, was all I needed. It may be unattainable, maybe unrealistic, but I was still on my quest to find out what this love was. I remember crying; praying as a little girl, asking God to please send someone to love me. I knew no one else to cry to, but to the Lord; feeling that deep down He could fix it. Many times, I cried that prayer, wondering why my mother didn't love me, why my father left me, why I was so unloved. Then I got pregnant at 14-years-old, expecting to produce something that would definitely love me, so I thought. I got out of one group home and came home to my mother. She was happy at first, but for me; I was determined to go my own path.

I was in the ninth grade when I met Jason, he was in the 12th grade, ROTC Navy bound. He would stare at me in the hallways, and even switched his classes in about a week of me being there. He was walking me to my classes, having lunch with me, even letting me wear his red Chicago Bull's starter jacket. It wasn't long after, that I would invite him in, while my mother and my sister weren't home. Even if Andrea had been there, it wouldn't have been an issue because she too had boys coming over. Indeed, she was sexually active at thirteen. I and Jason spent a lot of time together, talking in our little world. I was in love with him, and he loved me.

I eventually got kicked out of Garfield and had to go to Phoenix, the bad kids' school, because of my record and my two prior visits to D.Y.S. I was too much for regular school, my behavior was beyond control, and I was pregnant, so I was considered a risk. Jason signed up for the Navy. When I was finally delivered of Jessica, my daughter, in 1990, I was 15 and alone. I had to go through The Red Cross, just to get a message through to him. However, I talked to his mom regularly, as she also was awaiting her first grandchild. My mother, on the other hand, was getting me ready and prepared to have a baby as I was still living with her. My bedroom was set up as a baby-friendly spot, equipped with crib diapers and baby clothes; I was ready. My Mom was planning together with me, buying things; happy she was because she was expecting her first grandchild. Tragedy struck six weeks before my due date as I was lying in bed some morning, noticing my stomach tighten every few minutes. My mom being a nurse hesitated in taking me to the hospital, saying it wasn't true labor. I was 7-months pregnant, and something didn't feel right. Sure enough, shortly after reaching the hospital, we found out that I was in active labor, and I was dilated three centimeters. They stopped my labor, but it cost me three long weeks in the hospital. During the three weeks I was in the hospital, she rarely came to see me, and she accused me of having a bad attitude. Three weeks later, while at school, I would go to the bathroom only to see my mucous plug floating in the toilet. I went in full labor this time and delivered of a healthy baby girl at 12:26 am of Dec 4, 1990, even though she was early. She was a beautiful, healthy 6 pounds 9 ounces baby girl, and I couldn't take my eyes off her. I was excited, happy, and could hardly sleep. I was a mother, and I wanted to shout out at the top of my lungs! My mom stayed for the labor and delivery but left because she had to go to work in the morning.

Hours later, I finally got to sleep after feeding Jessica for the first time. I was awakened by nurses throughout the night and early morning hours. I was rudely awakened again a few hours later by two black women whom I would find out worked for the Summit County Children's Board; women who had been sent by my mother. My look of disgust and disapproval must have shown on my face because they pulled up a chair sat down and started talking, making me feel like this was serious. I was slightly angry with their attitude as they began to speak, so I sat up to hear just exactly what they wanted. They stated that my mother didn't think I would be able to care for my child, and that she wouldn't be able to help because she worked full time.

Since I was 15, it was outta my hands. When those women left, I somewhat panicked. Should I kidnap my baby because they made it crystal clear that when I left, I wasn't going to take my baby with me? I got on the phone and called the first person I needed to talk to; my mother, did she really betray me like this?

She was at work but when she answered and I asked her, she answered with her usual commentary, and had the nerve to say that after I work on myself, maybe then I can get her back, but that I could not bring her home with me. I hung up on her in the middle of her speaking. Forget her and forget that she was trying to ruin my life and shatter my dreams. Next on the list was my grandma Ann, she kept kids in foster care for a living. I begged her to please get my baby, since their plan was to adopt her out, and at the age of fifteen back then I had no rights. I couldn't stop them. My grandma promised me on the life of her dead son, my father, that she would get my daughter and that she would be there for me. Unfortunately, it was a process that did not come overnight. My next call was to Jason's mom, and upon telling her what happened, she let me know her chances of getting Jessica, were slim to none because of her felony history. I left the hospital two days later with no baby but caught the bus straight to Jason's mom's house. I stayed there a couple of days and eventually moved in around the corner with Jason's grandmother, but it really wasn't a party at her house. I wasn't back in school yet, so most of the time I just sat there and kept her company. I was just happy to be away from my mother, the person who continually hurt me, and I was determined never to go back there.

The most C.S.B. allowed me to do for Jessica, was to let me catch the bus to go see my baby girl weekly at C.S.B. On one of those visits, my grandmother Ann came with me, and we got to meet the foster parent; another older lady named Ms. McGowen, who knew my grandmother. They actually lived right around the corner from each other. From that point on, she allowed my grandmother to pick Jessica up from her house whenever she wanted, without C.S.B. She told my grandmother that before she realized that this was her family, her every intention was to adopt Jessica. Shortly after that, my grandmother got custody and she let me visit Jessica at her house whenever I wanted.

Unfortunately, that didn't keep me off the streets, and I ended up once again back in D.Y.S. for 90 days. This was my 3rd time since I was still on parole. After I got out, once again, I was back with my mom temporarily because they were looking for placement for me. This time, it was Lincoln Place in Youngstown, Ohio, an hour from Akron. In the few months I was there, Mom was constantly watching, constantly expecting me to mess up, and I was again on the verge of leaving. I wanted to go to the "next place." Any other place was better than her place. Eventually, my probation officer transported me to Youngstown, Ohio, to my new group home. I didn't have any expectation; I was just happy to be out of my mom's house.

Lincoln Place proved to be the best group home to me, centered in the heart of Youngstown, across the street from Youngstown State University. I was never locked up but felt more like a college student. We had our own room, a cafeteria, and pretty much could come and go during decent hours as we pleased. I was excited about being in a new place and meeting new people. Many of the girls I had previously been locked up with were there, and some from D.Y.S.; I felt right at home. The staff was cool more like friends, and before I could really meet any of the boys or men outside of the place,

I noticed one of the men watching me. He was 24 years old, and before I really hit the streets, he was taking me back and forth to his house. Of course, I never talked about those types of situations; I just learned to use them to my advantage. I received my perks and kept my mouth shut, not to mention I also had situations with girls from D.Y.S. No, I don't think I was gay, but I was an opportunist and was looking for any opportunity to be loved. To get attention is what I was really seeking, but I never found it. I stayed in contact with my grandma as far as Jessica was concerned. Even though I was still the way I was, she never once condemned me.

Jason, Jessica's father came home from boot camp to see about our daughter before he was stationed in Antigua. My grand-mother said he showed up, a fresh Navy man, on a mission to see his daughter. He was excited about being a father but wasn't ready, and neither was I. Whenever I got locked up, he wrote to me, but we were not together. Yes, we had a child and even talked about getting married, but he wasn't there physically, and I couldn't stay out of trouble, nor did I want to. It wasn't long after I arrived at my new placement with the help of the girls that were already there, I learned my way around this new city. I wanted to be pointed towards the hood; the bad part of town because that was the environment, I felt comfortable with.

It wasn't long before I found out or ran into what I was really looking for. He was 23 years old, but I was 15, and of course, I had lied about my age and told him that I was 19; a college student with a part-time job at a pizza shop. The pizza shop job was real; they let me sweep the floors, clean up, free pizza, and a few dollars here and there. I had earned this job just by going to the shop, running my mouth, and being talkative. Remembering how chatty I was as a kid, I learned how to get what I wanted by being extremely persuasive, wise, and even manipulative. Young boys wanted to talk, and I was all about that action. I met Ramel at a park, where I and my girls would frequently meet with boys and hang out; Wick Park to be exact.

We were just sitting there, looking cute, since our very purpose there was to meet boys and get into something. Ramel and a friend of his were shooting guns at the park. We were only being entertained by that, although that became our instant attraction. This man was handsome, a certified smooth talker, and knew all the right things to say at the right time and could buy alcohol. He was cool, and we got along, as he accepted me; I could be myself at least that is what I wanted to portray. He would sit at the pizza shop until I finished my work, and then we would spend time to-gether at the park where we met. We spent time together at his house when his mom wasn't there; I spent the night a few times, violating the rules of Lincoln Place.

I always came back though, even snuck back in through the window, or by the help of a friend. I wasn't trying to go back to jail. I felt I was in a good place, and I longed to be Jessica's mother soon. I had thoughts of working on myself, going to school and doing better. I just didn't know where to start. I was drawn to the worst of things, and bad company too. I literally searched for it, and Ramel satisfied that need in me. We had sex, we smoked, we drank, and ran around town regularly; that was our life. One day, he suggested we rob somebody since we didn't have any money to get high and party with. I didn't think twice about it since I was truly down for the cause. We were like Bonnie and Clyde on this night, and while we contemplated on whom to rob, we went and grabbed a couple of knives from his mom's house. We came back to sit at a location right around the college campus down the street from Lincoln Place; a heavy traffic area at night and someone was going to get caught slipping. Of course, I was rooting my man on, he didn't want me to be directly involved with the robbery, but he wanted me to have his back, just in case of any necessity. I was there with my knife. We waited and watched several people walk by, looking for just the right person to overpower, and of course they had to be alone. We sat there watching different people, as they walked by. Finally, our chance came by; a white guy a little older than us with a backpack walked right out of Burger King.

We waited a few minutes for him to pass us and then Ramel sprang into action. Ramel ran up on the man, put the knife in his back, and I sat there watching; thrilled. Things didn't work out like we had planned, as I saw them fighting from the distance they were. The man overpowered Ramel to the point where he had taken the knife from him. Ramel, I think, called out my name and I ran towards them. When I got there, they were both wrestling over the knife. I instinctively tried to help pry the knife from the man's hands, but he wasn't letting go. While they were still wrestling, I dropped my knife and took off running from them. I later ran back to Ramel's mom's house, but he was not there.

I waited for him to come praying he had got away, but he never came back. I eventually got back to where the robbery began. When I got there, I didn't see Ramel but was promptly met by the police. Yes, I was dumb for going back to the scene of the crime, but I was just fifteen and was looking for my boyfriend. I was informed that he was in jail, and that I was an accomplice. What I didn't know was that as I ran away from the scene, Ramel had stabbed this man five times in the abdomen and he was currently in the hospital waiting to see if he would pull through. I was on my way to the county jail, with the same charges, because I was involved. I didn't know how to feel at 15, I had a ten-month-old daughter, and I was being charged with attempted murder. I guess I got what I wanted because I never saw Ramel again. Once again, I was back in that place I hated, but facing adult charges this time.

Chg = attempted murder!!! went to jail

Jeremiah 29:11...

"For I know the plans I have for you, declares the Lord; plans to prosper you and not to harm you, plans to give you a hope and a future." [NLT]

_____

_____

_____

_____

_____

_____

Pray this prayer along with me:

Heavenly Father, ... though I may not know how things in my life are going to go, especially things I can't control, teach me to trust your views. Teach me to trust Your promise to me for my life, even though things naturally may be a mess in my life. I trust everything will work for my good... in Jesus' mighty name, Amen!

Chapter 2
"A Different Perspective"

The only way that doing time wasn't a waste of time, is if you become wiser, and learn more than what you knew before you went in. Learned from your mistakes and started life on a new path. You got to do your part and find a job; a place to stay and stay out of trouble. Sounds easy but imagine when you now have a stain on your record, that felony you spent time for; a record that's there for life. You leave jail pre-determined to fail, with doors that are already shut, and you haven't even knocked on yet. You must get your life right, but on top of the added stress you have to get life as you know it back to normal.

These are the 'what if' situations that jail doesn't factor in. The revolving door that some of us are drawn to. Nobody ever taught you how to lie or steal, it was suggested to you at a very young age, and you've been rolling with it ever since, just getting stronger and wiser. The total amount of time I got sentenced to was 18 months since they had changed the point system. I originally got 12 months, but due to this new point system, I got those extra points, which added time. I would spend a week in the County jail of Youngstown until my prints came back. These fools didn't even know I was a minor, and I didn't tell them anything. While I was there, I made a few phone calls, but my priority was finding out where my man was. I called Ramel's mom a few times to see what was up. She told me Ramel was in jail too. I called my grandma to check on Jessica a few times, but I never called my mom. I had the voice videotaped and pre-recorded in my mind, and I got tired of hearing it. I told myself that I didn't need her anymore, and the bitterness and unforgiveness towards her grew in my heart. When I talked to my grandmother, she informed me that my mom had the nerve to be visiting and picking up my Jessica. The last time, she took her to get her pictures taken and she brought her back with new clothes. I didn't care, though I felt like she shouldn't be visiting my child; the child that she made me leave at the hospital, especially when she never visited her.

Being in jail meant nothing doing, but reading and following the program, or go be gay to pass the time, and that came easily for the lonely ones; literally. School was mandatory in juvenile jail, and having a job was a privilege. Commissary and playing cards were what helped you tolerate the time you are given. Letters and phone calls were vital and were your only connection to the outside world. If you have a steady writer writing to you, you can play the tag game with them, a cycle that would help you deal with your time. I sat in the juvenile jail a couple of months, going back and forth to court, still in Youngstown, until I got sent back to D.Y.S. I met a friend there, her name was Jessica, just like my daughter and she was here for Murder One. She was on her way with me to that dreaded place, so I told her all about it. This was her first time but my fourth time, so I guess I was a vet to it, for real. Most of the girls from Ohio stuck together; Cleveland, Akron, and Youngstown, but the girls from Cincinnati, and Columbus there had something against us.

This place had their wake-up by 'five,' 'breakfast by six,' then their 'line up and walk to cafeteria.' Immediately after doing chores, we would be at school all day. Our time stayed structured, with groups and other activities that were all boring. We had gym time that was fun; we saw and worked out with the girls from other cottages. The highlight was the dances they would have ever so often with the boys from Riverview. If your behavior was up to par, you were able to go just like the dance at a local school.

Some of the boys knew us from the outside world, so the boys would claim us, and we would claim them too. After the dance would be over, we would write letters and stay connected. Then there was the library I chose to read to pass my time. I loved the way books made me feel on the inside. Besides reading books, Jason wrote to me regularly, and then Ramel started writing to me. They ended up giving him five to twenty-five years for that incident that we were both involved in, since he was an adult. We wrote regularly but the reality was that we were both locked up. Besides writing, we couldn't do anything else with each other.

Don't think I never for once thought about why I was there, and why I shouldn't be there. There was nothing he could say to stop making me feel some how about everything that went down. While I was there, I met a new staff member named Ms. Tucker. A lady that dressed, looked and acted like a man. When she walked by, she smelled like a man drenched in cologne. One day while at the gym Ms. Tucker just happened to be there, and while sitting on the bleachers, this girl that I had seen before, but barely knew, was sliding over to me. By signaling, she tried to tell me that Ms. Tucker liked me. I was shocked at first, my initial thought was, "wow," then, "why was she telling me this?" "What did she know?" What I discovered later was that she trusted this girl enough to pass the message through her, even though I wasn't gay. Though I was a straight-up opportunist, and down for whatever, I was curious as to why she liked me and what she had to offer. At any of the other times that I was there, I only participated in one gay activity, and that was on my second trip while in Buckeye. I had a roommate named Tina, a light-skinned pretty girl from Cleveland, Ohio, who was a little older than me. We were cool, got along, and often laughed at the gay girls around the campus, as well as their so-called relationships. One day, while

I was talking and standing by the window in our room, Tina walked over and kissed me. It was crazy, because by right, we should have been fighting, so I stood there shocked, feeling like what just happened.

Nevertheless, Tina became my girl until she left, and that was the end of that. Ms. Tucker eventually sent me a note through the same girl and attached to it was a piece of candy. We produced a fake name so she could write me and so she would send me boxes with the things I wanted. She sent money for my books and even had a bank account set up for me, and Jessica, pending when I get out. Our relationship went on like that for several months, writing back and forth, sending money and boxes until late one night when she opened my bedroom door and the game changed. I guess that was our 'one chance' since she was filling in for another staff member as she never worked on our unit. I didn't know how to feel about everything that had happened between us, considering this whole situation was on the downlow. I couldn't talk about it with anybody really, except maybe the girl that knew from the beginning. I told her how Ms. Tucker popped up in my room and what went down. I had to tell somebody, though while I was telling her she was telling someone else. Shortly after, I was questioned about Ms. Tucker. Our letters were confiscated, and a lot of things were under investigation. I was a regular conversation piece around the campus.

I was fed up with the questionings one day, and I got really angry. I was supposed to be going to school, but I slipped up and went to the building where Ms. Tucker worked. I ran up, knocked on the door, and she let me in. We talked briefly with plans to get me out of there. She quickly hid me in a laundry basket under a pile of dirty clothes. It would not be long before they discovered I was missing, and I had to produce a plan; a plan I needed to produce it immediately. She came to check on me a few times to make sure I was okay, but other than that it was business as usual.

Matthew 11:28...

"Come to ME, all you who are weary and burdened, and I will give you rest." [NLT}

_____

_____

_____

_____

_____

Pray this prayer along with me:

Heavenly Father, ...teach me how to deal with the hurt and the pain, then teach me how to use my pain as a steppingstone. Lead me into Your truth through Your word and the Holy Spirit. Let Your will be done for my life, and give me the wisdom to know the difference...

... in Jesus' mighty name, Amen!

Chapter 3
"Life, Still Goes On"

My grandma Ann did go out of her way once to visit me carrying Jessica. Jessica was walking and about 13-months-old, and she was so cute and precious to me. I hated that she had to see me in jail but looking back I was numb to it. Even though she was a baby and didn't fully understand, I regret it now though. I really didn't even think she knew I was her mother. The truth was all my running around in the streets trying to get high, chasing this boy, that man, should have come to an immediate screeching halt when I had Jessica, but I ran the other way. It was the pain, I know now; that drove me slowly away after I had her.

I left that day from the hospital without my daughter, but with pain whispering in my ear. I left with shattered dreams, disappointment, and my expectations for being a mother all gone. I began to blame myself for the way I acted, the running around, my actions like I didn't want a baby for real, like I didn't want her. Yes, I still loved Jason and dreamed of the plans made together. But I chose to ride with my pain, and I let it drive me deeper to more pain, and away from my daughter. I didn't know it then, but now I do. I was tricked by the pain; that he was not my friend. I couldn't see my future because I was tormented by my past. Running from the pain, with pain to more pain. Was I crazy? I was running physically, and I was running mentally to and from. Self-hatred began within me. My motivation for even living was gone, looking back at all that I had already lost; it was hard to continue. It was like nothing really mattered, just this intense need within me to run. I wasn't living life I was just going through the motions, running wild with no destination, running here, there and getting nowhere. I started missing my mom and Andrea a little bit, simply because I hadn't heard from them in a while. She and I were like Mutt and Jeff as our mom would often jokingly call us, but she was the closest thing to a twin to me. I took a chance to call and check on them; my mom did write, send boxes and some money on the regular. I called my mom's number, and it was disconnected. I didn't know what to think. I didn't find out until almost a month later that it was because of Andrea. She had the nerve to run up my mother's phone bill, talking to my man Ramel from jail, answering his collect calls, but hiding the bills. I was somewhat glad she FINALLY got busted, because honestly, I was always the one labeled the bad kid. Andrea was far from innocent, she did her dirt too, though she just looked good, doing it. Why was Ramel calling and talking to my little 14-year-old little sister when he was supposed to be my man? I quit talking to Ramel, and as for my sister when I finally did touchdown [get out] I never mentioned it.

Psalms 37:24...

"Though he may stumble, he will not fall, for the Lord upholds him with his hand."

[NLT]

Pray this prayer along with me:

Heavenly Father, ...as I read this book, turn my pain into the power of pain. Allow it to change me, for my benefit and for the benefit of others. Allow forgiveness to flood my heart and change me for your purpose. Help me to open my heart and mind to receive from You. Allow me to heal from my past, and let me move forward, and help others...

...in Jesus' mighty name, Amen!

Chapter 4
"Little Problems Big Consequences"

Ms. Tucker came by to check on me in the clothes basket one more time, about 10 pm. She got off work at 11:30, then her relief for the night would come. The staff were not allowed to park their cars directly at cottages. If they weren't trekking, they rode those small golf carts on campus. The personal cars had to be parked at the main staff office; the very first building you would find if you entered this place. It was only a 5–7-minute walk to any cottage convenient for the staff. I sat up to listen to Ms. Tucker make plans to pick me up and let me out of the building soon. Since she wanted to get off work at her regular time, she wanted to get off normally to pick me up somewhere down the road. This city Delaware, located in Ohio, considered Central Ohio, was located 30 miles away from the state's capital Columbus. There were almost no people here, no streetlights, very few houses, and then this place called Scioto Village D.Y.S. This dreadful place had been opened originally in October 1869 with 6 girls. The name then was State Reform and Industrial School. Their mission and purpose, "The reformation of exposed, helpless, evil, disposed and vicious girls." Incorrigible was added to the list as well, later though. Was that what I was, an evil child?

At this very moment, hiding in this clothes basket, with the boy's dirty laundry on top of me, I thought of every plan imaginable, and also of why I was so bad. While lying there, 6 hours until Ms. Tucker got off work, I even peed on myself. It wasn't like I was able to walk around in the boy's cottage, especially after I was being looked for because I was AWOL. She finally let me out around 15 minutes before she was scheduled to leave. She told me to run, hide and do anything necessary until she picked me up on the main road, which was Home Road.

There were very few houses on this street, barely any streetlights. Houses were miles apart and I was scared of going out in that dark pitched environment. I had no sense of time besides cars coming and going. I had no cell phone or watch to monitor time. I waited for what seemed like forever, because I saw her leave to go to her car. She just never came back. She left me, and I was still on campus an AWOL. I had to move, and I needed to use a phone ASAP. I started traveling down that dark road, ducking and dodging the very few cars that went by, I had become tired from this running and ducking, and I was angry. Ms. Tucker never came to get me. I was on my way back to Akron and there was nothing left to do. As I was walking, I saw a house with lights. I decided to investigate and peep through windows. I saw an older man sitting in his recliner, and he seemed to be alone. I had to think fast, get my plan and story together, knocked on the door, and at that moment my lie all came together. I told him while he answered, "My car stopped down the road and I needed to use your phone." The frail, white-haired man shook his head and said, "sure," as he led me in, and pointed to his phone. My only intention there was to use the phone and nothing else, until I saw the keys to his car sitting plain as day on the table. I didn't know how to drive. I never drove at 16, but that did not stop me from trying though. I sat there for 3 hours pretending to be waiting for rescue. I called Ms. Tucker, but she answered and said she couldn't pick me up, because she claimed they were watching her. I started calling friends and people who may possibly be able to pick me up. The man now desired that I should leave, I had worn out my welcome. When I left his house, I took his keys with me as I got up and walked out his door. When I walked out, I noticed he had two cars in his driveway a van and a grey Cadillac. The van was first, and the Cadillac parked behind it. I ran for the Cadillac. The door was open. I briefly looked back at his door to make sure he wasn't watching, then slipped right in the car door. The first car key I tried worked as I fumbled in the dark for the ignition. The lights came on as I started the car. This was my very first-time driving. I didn't know what to do next, so I put the car in drive, and I bumped the van in front of me because I had stepped on the gas. I hit the van so hard that the man started yelling from his door. He must have heard the sound of the collision. I don't think I even turned the car off when I got out to run. I ran until I saw a pay phone to call Scioto Village collect to tell them I needed to turn myself in. I had been AWOL for 13 hours. First girl to ever ac-complish that ever since it had been called Scioto Village in 1965. When they were picking me up on Home Rd, I realized many con-sequences awaited me, I just didn't know which ones they were. Either way, I had to be ready to take all of them for my actions. Nobody ever ran away from here, not one time had I heard of it. Girls did their time and got out but not me. As I was led back in the staff office, I heard the deputies ask what to do with me.

Daniel 9:9...

"The Lord our God is merciful and forgiving, even though we have rebelled

against Him." [NLT]

Pray this prayer along with me:

Heavenly Father, as I read this book, turn my pressure and pain into the power of pain, allow it to change me, for my benefit and for the benefit of others... by the power of your Holy Spirit. Allow forgiveness to flood my heart, change me for your purpose, and allow me to make a choice to use this pain for my benefit, and re-lease it to You! Open my heart and mind to receive from You and allow me to heal from my past. Allow me to move forward, and help others...

... in Jesus' mighty name, Amen!

Chapter 5
"The End of My Tunnel"

U p until this point in my life, all things have ended up as an epic failure. There were some things that seemed to be influencing my motives constantly and my actions too. I thought about God, and all the things I had learned about Him in church as a child but then I realized that I didn't know Him. Even when I attended church in here at D.Y.S. on Sundays and read my bible too, I still did not understand why I could not reach God and why He didn't change me; make my life better. I decided in my mind right then about God. Since He had not been helping me thus far, I probably didn't need Him now.

I placed Him in the same category with everyone else that did me wrong including my mom, my dad, Ms. Tucker and everyone else. Right now, I can't look at things the way I did then. I know better now. His promises in the Word are concrete, and His ways change not. The big difference in my thinking from then until now is my perspective and how I processed. Perspective is a word people use often without knowing the meaning. It is an attitude toward or a way of regarding something a point of view according to Webster's dictionary. Everyone has their own perspective and that is why we all differ. Also, our perspective changes as we gain wisdom, experience and just grow older.

I literally made up my mind at age sixteen, that God hated me and had abandoned me. I began to hate myself. If I wanted to live, I had to change and get better.

Deuteronomy 31:8, "It is the Lord that goes before you. He will be with you; He will not leave or forsake you. Do not fear or be dismayed." [KJV]

If He did promise to never leave or forsake you, then you were the one who left Him. Through sin, and constant disobedience, I left Him. I was given an extra six months for escaping from D.Y.S. I was sent here for 16 months for a crime I never committed but was dumb enough to be affiliated with someone who did. I never saw Ms. Tucker again, and at this point we were still actively under investigation. I was questioned numerous times about the letters and the nature of our relationship. I was mad at her still, for not coming to pick me up, so I told the truth. I no longer cared about protecting her, because in my book she had betrayed me. I only had five months left on my sentence the day I ran from that place, but at that moment I began to look at 11 more months; almost another year, thanks to my dumb decisions. Ms. Tucker also ended up losing her job at D.Y.S. and was sent to prison for statutory rape. She had to register for life as a sex offender. I testified against her, the letters were way too incriminating once they found out her alias, so there was no room to lie. I wasn't gay either, but I loved attention and was an opportunist. [someone who immediately takes advantage of a situation to reap some personal benefits.] I was numb, not feeling the pain anymore, ignoring its presence and refusing to think about it anymore, then eventually I would forget about it like it never happened. At least that was the plan. I spent my next few months out of trouble, but my head in a book.

My stay had been extended but I could not afford for it to be extended any further. I spent all off my time reading and listening to gospel music. My favorite song was "Ain't no need to worry", by Anita Baker and the Winans. It promised me something mentally as I sang the lyrics; "Ain't no need to worry, what the night is gonna bring, because it'll be all over in the morning." Somehow faith in God was birthed within me or rather restored within me at that point. He gives each one of us our own measure of faith, according to Romans 12:3. Does that mean we all have a different amount? Only God knows. Though, I do know according to this verse that we were all given a measure.

From listening to certain songs listening and meditating on them, I began to remember my childhood, when I listened to Sis. Tyler my Sunday school teacher tell us children about Jesus. It was all connected. I started praying and asking God to change me. I began to make sure that I was at many church functions. When people from local churches would come to fellowship with us, I would enjoy their visits. The time they spent with us, the snack, the special privileges, and special attention. I was finally starting to see, maybe not understand fully, but see, and my eyes were getting open.

I was not a stranger to church, for that was my foundation. As a little girl, going back and forth the group homes and jail; most of them make Church a requirement. I grew up in sanctified churches; apostolic church, with people shouting [dancing in the Spirit], and speaking in tongues. Don't get caught laughing, or you got the look, like you wish you hadn't, and pinched. Mothers had a way, back when I was growing up to look at you that way and you would stop in mid-air what you are doing. Even though we always went to those anointed churches, I had never seen my mom act like that. She never spoke in tongues, and she never shouted. With this new behavior I was displaying I was getting noticed, by the staff and some of those girls. I was scheduled to be released in March, back to my mother three months earlier than planned. They took three months off for good behavior. After serving 19 long months, it was time to go. I was being released.

Proverbs 3:5-6 ...

"Trust in the LORD with all thine heart; and lean not unto thine own understanding.[6] In all thy ways acknowledge him, and he shall direct thy paths." [KJV]

_____

_____

_____

_____

_____

_____

Pray this prayer along with me:

Heavenly Father, as I read this book, turn my pressure and pain into the power of pain, allow it to change me, for my benefit and for the benefit of others ... by the power of your Holy Spirit. Allow forgiveness to flood my heart, change me for your purpose, and allow me to make a choice to use this pain for my benefit, and re-lease it to You! Open my heart and mind to receive from You, al-low me to heal from my past, allow me to move forward, and help others ...

... in Jesus' mighty name, Amen!

Chapter 6
"My New Beginning"

After I got off that long 4-hour Greyhound bus ride home, I thought about my life and hoping better days were ahead of me. I was hopeful as I stepped off the bus to walk over to my mom, who was waiting for me. I wanted things to work out with us because I truly loved my mom and my sister too. I was determined to work on myself this time, because honestly after this last trip to D.Y.S. I knew it would be my last. I was getting ready to be eighteen in less than 2 months. No more kiddie jail for me. My next trip was going to be at the Summit County Jail, and no more juvenile courts. All these stains; these felonies I got in my youth would be sealed up, but the adult record never goes away.

When I got home, I exhaled fresh air. I was finally back in Akron and around every place that was familiar. I was free! I could not wait to lay in my bed in my own room; the little things I missed while being in jail. We all went out to eat the first night at Parrasons, an Italian restaurant. Then we went back home, watched a movie, and I sat and talked to my mom. I was finally tired from running the streets and being locked up. I just wanted to live, somehow be happy and be loved by my mother. When I turned eighteen, the plan was for my grandma Ann to transfer custody of Jessica to me. I saw my baby girl the next day. She was almost three now, but when I went to jail, she wasn't even a year old. Now, I was staring at a toddler; my grandmother took great care of her, but she was spoiled. I started school again at Garfield H.S. as a senior, but I had a few credits to make up for. I started Night School to graduate from my class on time. I honestly felt like an adult already since most of my childhood had been spent in one institution or another. I loved my new job; my new schedule of things to do, and my life seemed to be coming together slowly but surely. I enrolled in parenting classes in downtown Akron at A.P.S., a Pregnancy Resource Center. A Christian Organization designed as an outreach to pregnant women. The services were free, and they also gave free pregnancy tests. This was the place I went to get my pregnancy test at 14, when I suspected I might be pregnant, and also, they don't notify parents. They pray with you, help you evaluate your situation, and then offer you the resources you need to be successful. Then there were the awesome classes they offered for parenting, domestic violence, self-development, and spiritual nuggets, still all free of charge. They had baby clothes, diapers, and the formula which they gave away all for free. The cool thing about the classes was that as you attended, you earned vouchers towards furniture for your baby like cribs, car seats and playpens.

The volunteers at that Akron Pregnancy Center were the nicest people I knew. They showed genuine love to me, and they were the first people who reminded me what the bible said about love. They gave me a glance at how God expressed it. That was something I often wondered about, 'the church was associated with God, but the church is only ran by man, and man is capable of mistakes, but God never made mistakes and He dwelt in a true believer, not in buildings.'

Acts 8:48, "However, the Most High [the One infinitely exalted above humanity] does not dwell in houses made by human hands as the prophet [Isaiah] says ..." [AMP]

The church [spiritually] represents Jesus Christ's [Yeshua Hamashiac, Hebrew] Bride, the bride of Christ.

Ephesians 5: 25-27, "Husbands, love your wives [seek the highest good for her and surround her with a caring unselfish love] just as Christ also loved the church and gave Himself up for her so that HE might sanctify the church, having cleansed her by the washing of water with the word [of God] .so that [in turn] He might present the church to Himself, in glorious splendor, without spot or wrinkle or any such thing; but that she would be holy [set apart for God] and blameless."

Many in the church do not take that step towards HOLINESS, which as you see, is a requirement to see Christ. Many members and leaders bring sinful ways and motives with them. The church becoming a place to exalt themselves, and not God. If you are in Christ, you should represent Him by your actions and your obedience, and holiness is a requirement.

Matthew 7:21-23 ESV "Not everyone who says to me 'Lord, Lord' will enter the kingdom of heaven, but the one who does the will of my Father who is in heaven. On that day many will say to me, Lord, Lord did we not prophesy in your name, and cast out demons in your name, and do many mighty works in your name? And then will I declare to them, 'I never knew you; depart from me, you workers of lawlessness."

John 8:44

..."You belong to your father, the devil, and you want to carry out your father's desires. He was a murderer from the beginning, not holding to the truth, for there is no truth in him. ... He was a murderer from the beginning, and does not stand in the truth, because there is no truth in him."

[NIV]

_____

_____

_____

_____

_____

_____

Pray this prayer along with me:

Heavenly Father, As I read this book, turn my pressure and pain into the power of pain, allow it to change me, for my benefit and for the benefit of others... by the power of your Holy Spirit. Allow forgiveness to flood my heart, change me for your purpose, and allow me to make a choice to use this pain for my benefit, and release it to You! Open my heart and mind to receive from You, allow me to heal from my past, allow me to move forward, and help others...

...in Jesus' mighty name, Amen!

Chapter 7
"On My Own"

I was seeing my daughter Jessica so regularly that she practically lived at my mom's house with us. My daughter, I felt was my responsibility and that I could carry it. I was going to night school and attending parenting classes. I was really busy, having no time to waste, but then, I let my guard down and got distracted by my weakness, men. Honestly, my real weakness probably was the attention and affection that I lacked growing up. I met Jeff walking down the stairs at night school, on my way to my class. Jeff was 19 and went to Buchtel High school. Jeff was persistent, and almost relentless about getting my attention and getting my phone number which actually was the main reason I gave it to him. We started hanging out immediately after his initial phone call. He came and picked me and my daughter, Jessica, in his car and we would ride around. Jeff also had a daughter named Jeffa, who was probably six months older than Jessica and he would bring her around sometimes. His baby's mother soon found out about me and Jeff and was so angry that she set out to break us up. I didn't understand it then, but I do know now that she was hurting over not being with her baby's dad. If he could make it work with me, he should be able to make it work with her and their child. Jeff took me around and introduced me to his family. I met his mother and came to find out that she actually went to my family's church and that she knew my family. No matter how nice she was, I don't think she thought I was good enough for her son. Jeff I could tell, was a momma's boy. He listened to her, valued her opinions, and still lived with her; I couldn't compete with that.

Jeff had a job working on cars with his uncles; they had their own automobile repair shop. We both worked and had ambition; reaching towards our goals, but I had no idea where our relationship was heading. I really liked him, loved spending time with him, and felt he made me happy. We never argued or fought, and we got along good with each other. We were about to graduate in June, but shortly after my 18th birthday, I found out I was pregnant with baby number two. Me, Jeff and our parents decided we should find our own place, and they were willing to help us. My mother and Jeff's mother paid our first month's rent and security deposit to our very own first apartment.

We rented an apartment, on the bottom floor, with the full use of the basement. To get us started, our parents gave us some starter furniture, a bed, a dresser, and a few things for us to sit on. We were both working and going to school, but things started changing between us. I began to see the real him; jealous, and insecure. I caught Jeff in many different lies, most times about very stupid stuff, and I was starting to lose interest. I started wondering if all this was a mistake; him and the baby I was carrying.

Since I got home in March, I was working really hard in school. I wanted to graduate and go on to college. I didn't have a specific job in mind, or what courses I wanted to take. Anything was good enough for me to do what I needed to do for me and mine. I was leaning towards the medical field because my mom was an R.N., and no matter what, I looked up to her. Since this was my senior year, I had planned to go to the prom, I had to be there, but I did not have a date. Jeff said he wasn't going; he was graduating from a different high school and had his own prom to go to but didn't go to either.

I asked my new friend Trina if she could suggest a date for me, and my girl came through. His name was Chris, and even though he attended another school, he needed a date also. He paid for everything the tickets and my corsage. We danced, we ate and took some awesome prom pictures. After the prom, I made it clear to Chris that I needed to go straight home and not to the hotel, like the rest of the seniors. We were not at all romantically involved, though he was a nice guy, a good friend. He dropped me off at my apartment to my boyfriend, who was waiting up for me. As I walked in, Jeff was lying in bed watching T.V. He looked up at me as I walked in like a suspect; like one who had done something wrong. Jeff stared at me while I got undressed, and after a minute asked me about the prom, and what we did? I snapped out a reply, headed to the room, got in on my side of the bed, and went straight to sleep. I honestly felt some type of way about him not going to the prom with me, and I didn't want to talk. Jeff was childish to me, and as far as my relationship with him was concerned, I was tired.

I started hanging out with my friends more as it was approaching graduation time. We would get frequent at the bar the Double-Time, around the corner from my house. Trina' was into older men, and since she was my road dog, I was looking at them too. I had my own issues that I was becoming aware of; I thought the world should pause and revolve around me. I could not stand to be told no, and if you didn't give me the attention, I felt I deserved, I moved on to someone who would. It has always been my way or the highway, and that was the way I treated men; like they owed me something. I made them pay for losing my dad and everything else that I had lost. I was determined to use what someone wanted from me as a benefit.

Through my girl Trina' I got introduced to a man named Bryce, who was older than me and was a big-time dope-dealer. We started having arrangements "sexually" that benefitted both of us. I even invited him to me and Jeff's apartment, while Jeff was not there. When we were not at school or working, me and Jeff would smoke weed hang out with our neighbors or have them hang out at our house. One night, I was drinking with my neighbors and Bryce called me, saying he wanted to see me, and Jeff just happened not to be there. I was light weight drunk, not thinking about the fact that if Bryce came over, Jeff still had a key. I let him come over anyways, and as we were sitting on the couch making out, all of a sudden, I heard the doorknob turn and keys jingling; Jeff was here. I jumped off the couch and tried to prevent him from seeing what I had done, but it was too late. He opened the door before I got there and saw me with Bryce. He walked away, didn't say anything; just walked out the door and left me standing there.

After that day things were never the same. After he walked in to see me and Bryce, he summoned the nerve to hit me a couple of days later. I called the police on him immediately. Domestic Violence was the charge, and he never did one day in jail for it. Jeff questioned me over and over about whose baby I was really carrying, after Bryce and that whole situation played out. Jeff did come back home that night, and yes, I felt bad for getting caught, not exactly for what I did though. I had to answer questions and questions, and for the most part I kept it real. I was already busted so there was no reason to really lie. The truth was that I was drunk, and I made a bad decision, leaving out the part that I knew him, and this was not his first time at our house. I never saw Bryce on that level anymore. It was over, and I could just imagine his impression of me after I just got him caught up in a situation like that. I never felt like he was impressed with me anyways. I was young to him, and I was naive. I found out later, about two weeks before graduation that I could not walk and get my diploma with my class, and that I had missed two parts of the Ohio Proficiency Test which were required for all 9th graders:

math and social studies which were my two worst subjects. Why were they just telling me now when nothing could be done? Now, my world was literally crushed. They also said that I had violated the attendance policy by barely going to do just enough work to make it by.

Zechariahs 4:6

"'Not by might nor by power, but by my Spirit' says the Lord God Almighty." [NLT]

_____

_____

_____

_____

_____

_____

Pray this prayer:

Heavenly Father, as I read this book, turn my pressure and pain into the power of pain, allow it to change me, for my benefit and for the benefit of others ... by the power of your Holy Spirit. Allow forgiveness to flood my heart, change me for your purpose, and allow me to make a choice to use this pain for my benefit, and release it to You! Open my heart and mind to receive from You, allow me to heal from my past, allow me to move forward, and help others...

... in Jesus' mighty name, Amen!

Chapter 8
"Where I first Started"

I could not stand the smell of chicken frying while I was pregnant, it made me nauseated and at almost three months pregnant, my job at KFC had to go. I liked the job and had done almost every job there. I knew what I was doing and knew how not to ring up food in order to hook people up. At night when we were closing, I would see them throw trays and trays of biscuits and chicken that people didn't buy by the end of the night. Every now and then they would let us take as much as we wanted home to our own families. Even when the uncool managers worked, we still took food, and I was one of them; we needed it. We could be low on food, me and Jeff.

My mom religiously paid her bills and mortgage but other than that, we were on our own. Mom was a bit of a hoarder too; she shopped at the thrift store regularly and bought things excessively, including things she didn't need. I had to make adult decisions for the household and for my sister, when she was gone. I was the oldest, but I lacked making good choices concerning my own life and where I was headed. I needed somewhere to stay after the fighting, arguing and Jeff hitting me. My mom suggested I come back home until I could make a new plan for myself, Jessica and the new baby. My new plan was to sign up for low-income housing, get my own place for me and my babies, and get up out my mom's house as soon as possible. Surprisingly, things were not at all that bad, besides my mom's sudden hospital trips for a week here and there. Things were at peace.

Did I worry about my mother? Yes, it crossed my mind since I didn't understand this "mental issue" she had. I didn't understand what caused her to repeatedly go in and out of the hospital. I couldn't understand why she was so depressed and unhappy. I always thought it was because of me. She often came home and would share her work experiences with me and Andrea. How patients would become combative and the different things she went through at work. It was my mom's knowledge, the years of schooling, and the on-the-job training that alerted her of her own problems, I think. It caused her to seek help for herself.

At my mom's house, after all that we had been through eventually, I and Jeff got back together. The reality was I was getting ready to have our child, and that wasn't going to change. I decided my child needed a father. My expectations of Jeff were simple; I wanted him to be a father to our child. We were still trying to be together, but those phone calls from Jeff's ex were getting ridiculous. She was extremely mad, finding out he had a new baby on the way by somebody else. It didn't help that deep down he was still unsure about the baby I was carrying, because when we would argue, that would always be the first thing he would bring up. I understood his reservations, yes, I messed up, and how was he to know this wasn't my regular scheduled program? i.e., how I truly was. I could accept that, and I knew the only way to prove myself was to have the baby so he could see for himself.

I got the keys to my new apartment shortly thereafter, but I didn't officially move in until after I had my baby. It was wintertime in Ohio, cold, and snowing outside, and my mom suggested I just stay close to her. My new apartment was in Barberton, Ohio an outskirt of Akron. I was 7-months pregnant with no car, and a 4-year-old daughter. Yes, my grandmother gave me custody of my little girl back. Everything came together with my new place and with my baby. I was thankful to my grandmother for raising her and taking good care of her. We didn't hear from Jason, and eventually, we stopped hearing from him altogether. He eventually married someone else and settled in Virginia. Still in the Navy, he moved on with his life just as I had with Jeff and my new baby. I was delivered of my baby prematurely at 34 weeks, due to listening to someone's baby advice about Castor Oil. I drank a half bottle of castor oil, was in the bathroom for hours when the contractions started. I barely made it to the hospital; I had Monica within 45 minutes of arriving to the hospital. Monica my second child, was born January 1994 weighing only 5'14 she had to be immediately rushed to ICU due to breathing difficulties. My mother and Jeff were in the delivery room. Jeff's mother came up to the hospital to view the baby and told me, Jeff and my mother that my baby didn't look like Jeff. I decided then his mother wasn't right, who would say such foolish thing right after I got delivered. I felt pressured mentally, just desiring to prove to Jeff that this was his baby, based on the things he said to me when he got angry at me. My mom spoke up at that moment on my behalf, saying we were going to get a test to prove it. She also spoke up to say, she was sure about my baby being her granddaughter. About a month later, I got a letter in the mail to start the paternity proceedings for Jeff. We all had to go down there to get blood work drawn. Monica only had to stay an additional ten days in the hospital to get her lungs strong, eat, and pick up weight. She still was considered a premature baby and still required a lot of attention. Those test results came back when Monica was 2 months old and it read that Jeff was the father, according to DNA probability of 99.99 percent compatibility, so I won just like that!

In that moment, it occurred to me that beauty has a flaw some small hidden imperfection, mostly invisible to the naked eye. I realize much of my life was just like that, bitter and angry on the inside while beautiful on the outside, appearing well put together. I often cried out to God because I was tired of the pain and couldn't keep away from it...

Jeremiah 6:16...

"This is what the Lord says "Stand at the crossroads and look; ask for the ancient paths ask where the good way is and walk in it and you will find rest for your souls. But you said, 'We will not walk in it.'" [NIV]

_____

_____

_____

_____

_____

_____

Pray this prayer:

Heavenly Father You said If we trust in You with all our hearts You shall direct our paths, please lead and guide us and don't let us be led by our emotions. Keep our minds and hearts focused directly on you, so we shall know which way to go. Lead us away from temptation in Jesus' name Amen. (Praise God, and believe in your heart, and He will guide you).

...in Jesus' mighty name, Amen!

Chapter 9
"My Cold Heart"

I was a full-time mother of two children now, when a few months ago I wasn't even responsible for any. I loved my kids so much and I did not want to fail as a mother. Before Jessica was in my custody, I was more of a babysitter to her than a mother, but now I had them both at the same time. Monica was a handful. If I weren't holding her, she was crying, and I would admit I wasn't ready for this part of parenting. I was overwhelmed with that constant crying. She was still considered a premature baby and all she wanted was to be comforted and loved. I thank God that period didn't last long. It was at about 5 months when she stopped crying and was just a happy baby. I dressed Monica and Jessica like twins even though they weren't. I bought two of everything and thought my little girls looked so cute matching and all. Monica loved music and loved to dance and was often sighted waving her hands to the music from her highchair. Monica had a smile that lit up the room and just made you smile; her smile was just like her father's. Jessica was quiet and was like any other toddler who wanted to watch cartoons and play with her toys. My next-door neighbor was a lady named Nikki, who was just a little bit older than me. I and Nikki clicked immediately. I admired and looked up to her like a big sister. Our original connection was because we were neighbors, but she also had a 4-year-old daughter that my daughter Jessica could play with.

Nikki taught me a lot about being a woman, and how to function with the men out there. She even taught me how to experience pleasure during sex. Even though I had two kids, I had never experienced it, but then she taught me about life in a different aspect. I wasn't just listening to Nikki, I was also paying attention, mentally soaking it all in, just like a child. I saw the men she entertained, the beautiful apartment she had, and the way she treated her daughter. I strongly took her pieces of advice when it came to men; when she told me not to be running around having sex for no money with nothing to show for it. I had learned how to respect my body and to keep my goods to myself unless I could receive some gain from it. As I learned to function like this, my heart turned cold, love no longer was my goal. Nikki helped me get through the crying stage with Monica. She would come over, grab Monica's bassinet and take her for the night to give me a break, and I appreciated her for that. Jeff by the way, offered very little support in raising our child and in financially supporting us. He had no problem sliding through, eating my food, having sex with me, and running out on me when my check was low. Nikki helped me recognize that after several months of letting me down, it became clear he wasn't going to keep his obligation to his daughter, and I was wasting my time on him. I made Jeff pay whenever he would come around and desire to have sex with me. He had money and he knew my requirements. Besides, he never bought clothes, diapers or food. I felt I was responsible to get everything from him in the best way I could. Jeff worked sometimes, but he spent the majority of his money buying weed and working on cars. He still stayed with his mama, and she had very little contact with me, and no communication at all with her granddaughter. She never visited or even acknowledged ownership of her grandchild after the paternity test. I really felt in my heart that she was mad about being wrong. I wasn't going away, and neither was my daughter.

Since my father had died, my mother had been collecting survivor's benefits for I and Andrea. I had heard it spoken multiple times that she was money hungry, but I didn't understand that. I also could not understand why she allowed my social security benefits from my dad to discontinue after I turned 18. I was still eligible for two months after my 19th birthday, and for my children this was the first piece of real business I had to take care of. My grandmother Ann, my dad's mom told me how he made it his business to fill out paperwork to ensure his children were taken care of in case of an emergency. I got my first back check from social security a couple of weeks before I moved to Barberton. I used that to buy furniture and things for my children. I and mom's relationship kept deteriorating, and instead of being a mother and providing direction, she was more of a taskmaster. Whenever she visited me or my kids, she never told me how to be a good parent, she rather chose to put me down and tell me how terrible a parent I was. Her main complaint about me was that I slept all day, but I had been up all night with Monica. It was hard to accept any criticism from her; in the unloving, hateful way she said it. My mom did not like Jeff, she criticized our relationship, and always refused to help. I had begun seeing other men, and Jeff could not take it. I think it was because of the new friends that he had. There was a crew of these dudes he now was hanging around with, and they were all related in some type of way. What I didn't understand was why they were hanging out with Jeff. These men worked and hustled, drove nice cars, and got money. This new behavior Jeff was displaying involved guns, kicking in my door if I didn't answer and threatening any other man who was over my house. Letting any man know he was my baby's father, and back then I thought it was funny, and if I remember quite clearly, I really thought he cared. But then, Jeff out here acting a fool, pulling guns out on other men, kicking my whole door off the hinges, the entire scenario got old quick. I came home once to meet him in my house, and I tried to let him out forever. Akron Metropolitan Housing Authority would kick people out for destroying property; he had to stop. This was my apartment, and it belonged to me and my two daughters. It was turning into a flophouse for Jeff, his friends, and my girls. Since I had been living in the Norton Homes community, I met and ran into many people. Carla who lived behind me with her sister Shannon, frequently would spend the night at my house. We smoked, drank, and met many men together; this was my homegirl for real. Then there was Evonne, who lived in the building next to me, one of the coolest white girls I had ever met in my life. Evonne messed around with only black men.

I visited Evonne's house daily; I and my two kids, either partying or hooking up with somebody. I remember me and Evonne had gotten a hold of a Ouija board one time, and we got curious. After getting drunk and high one night, we pulled out the board. We put our hands on it, expecting it to move, but most of the time we would look at each other until one night it moved! We both looked at each other in amazement as we felt the gentle pull, while we asked it answered Evonne seemed to get a message from her grandfather, but it scared us both, mostly because what was said was true. We both got scared and decided we would never play with it again. I mean we were really shaken up, praying and calling prayer lines. Me and my girl Evonne were literally scared of what the devil might do to us. We both had God-fearing backgrounds, growing up in church setting, so something within us knew it was wrong. I dibbled and dabbled in the dark side before being around the different kids, the different walks of life, and with the different group homes. I remember being in Oesterlen when I was thirteen; a couple of kids I knew there were drawing pictures with Satan rules on it. One particular boy there named Derrick liked me and we dated a little while. With Derrick and his friends (my so-called new friends), I was intrigued by them. They had a hateful view of God because they felt that He had in some way let them down and they were hurt, abused, and confused. I sat there while they put God down, burned bible pages, and acted out in anger. I never really participated with them, but since I was there, I was an accomplice to a crime in the eyes of the law. I expressed my belief in God to Derrick, but in my heart, I felt that God had abandoned me just like my parents. I didn't share that same hate for God as they had, but I was confused because I felt I didn't matter. I didn't hate Him even though I thought He hated me. I was just not entirely cool with this and with Derrick, so we soon broke up after that.

I and Nikki went out a lot to bars and clubs in Cleveland, Ohio. She taught me how to dress, put makeup on, and attract the type of men that had money. She might not have realized that she was teaching me something, but I was taking notes. She told me I shouldn't be having sex for free, especially if I was in lack in any way. I started seeking older men and to notice the way they treated me, and how they loved to spend money on me. I met one in Barberton; he was dark-skinned, bald with one gold open-faced tooth in front. His name was Earl, and he was married. He rarely rode me around town in his Cadillac because of his wife. I was a "creep" person very few people knew about, and if I was getting his money, none of his business was my concern. There was a lesbian couple who lived in my community and that reminded me of my recent past relationship with Ms. Tucker. Seeing them together got me curious again, but I didn't have relationships, just relations. I met a girl through one of my new friends, and one off a chat line, but it was all just fun; hardly anybody knew until I met Cora. The only reason everybody in my friend circle knew was because I brought her home from the club. One night I and Nikki went out to a lesbian bar in Cleveland, this was our second or third visit to this club. I loved the atmosphere, gay men, and black lesbians being themselves.

I didn't hook up with anybody these last times that me and Nikki went out. I danced with and passed out a number, but that was it until this night. I didn't meet Cora inside the club but at the parking lot. Herself and one other female were there fighting, but Cora caught my eye. Short light-skinned, stocky with a box haircut and a curly shag in the back. I think we were instantly attracted, and I was just being nosy, staring at her across the parking lot, as she was loudly arguing with another girl. I remember seeing her in the club; a lightweight girl staring at me I thought to myself. They eventually pulled off together, we did too, only to get down the street to see Cora walking and no car in sight. We pulled over to ask if she was alright. As we pulled up, we could see she had obviously been in a fight. Her shirt was stretched, her hair messed up. She said she needed a ride, but she had nowhere to go and that she wanted to go with us. It was a crazy two-week ride with Cora; she left my house in handcuffs and got some years for burning my neighbors' apartment up. She was an alcoholic, and I should have left her that day walking in Cleveland. After that, I never heard from her again. Carla, my best friend began staying with me, she had a guy named Fred whom she was seeing. He came over with his friend and his ride. G-Money was how he introduced himself to me. He had such a deep, baritone voice, almost like a smooth midnight DJ voice on the radio. He was cute and chubby, but not my type. He was quiet and didn't really talk much.

He was dark-skinned and had braids. I could tell he was a hus-tler by the way, he dressed and carried himself. I didn't flaunt all over him, and he didn't seem interested in me. Fred and G became frequents to my house, and I enjoyed their company. Over the next few weeks of them coming over, G started talking to me more. I think our ice breaker was when G dropped some money at my house, and instead of keeping it, I gave it to him. I mean we played cards, we watched movies, smoked and drank together, but it was nothing like talking one-on-one. I was intrigued by the fact that G was not all up on me, or maybe because I was just used to that. G was different. I could tell he wasn't from around here. I came to find out he was from the D (Detroit); born and raised. Raised by his grandma, and had nothing but sisters, then on top of that, he had two daughters. I could tell he had an advantage on how to treat women, but I wanted to know why he left the D to move here. I stereo-typed G because of what I knew and experienced in the past. He was obviously selling dope and kept wads of money. Whenever he lifted his shirt slightly, I saw his pistol. G gave me his pager number and told me to page him whenever I wanted to get out to do something. This was 1995, cell phones with ridiculous prices. I didn't have a house phone.

After my check from my dad ran out when I was 19, I had to get assistance for me and the kids. I didn't have any money for the day-to-day things where you had a new outfit, a new attitude, and a couple of dollars in your pocket. Very few people had a phone and most of us who lived there went across the parking lot to the laundromat, to use the payphone. We didn't waste our money on weed and alcohol; that was the main reason we had the men coming by the house. Back then you didn't really have to buy it; somebody always had it and they wanted to party.

I met some Christian people out there, but I hadn't found a church yet, so I would watch shows like the 700 club and the church channel. I still had a deep longing for Him, and I couldn't quite explain the void and emptiness I felt on the inside. I remembered my childhood and the way my mother treated me, but for the most part, I just wanted to forget. My mom called C.S.B. on me and told them I sleep all day and don't take care of my kids. I got so angry at her once again for meddling with my life. I told my mom to stay out of my business and kid's life. These same people whom she had got me involved with when I had Jessica, she got these people back in my life. Nothing ever came of it, they never took the kids, but the fact that they were aggravating me and checking up on me did drive a wedge between me and my mother. My mom swore to never get involved with my kids again. She tried to keep her promise until the day she passed away. I did have a couple of incidents involving Jessica and those were not my fault. One was when Jeff was putting Jessica in the bathtub, and it was filled with hot water; the skin was peeled off her foot. Then another incident was with Jessica's grandma (Jason's mother) who kept the kids when I worked and needed a break. On one of those visits, she took a straightened comb to try to do Jessica's hair and apparently it didn't go well. Jessica did not sit still, and she came home with burns on her hand and a few on her scalp. I got blamed for both incidents, and of course, you know who the reporting officer was, my mother. I cut her off and didn't want any dealings with her after that.

One of my Christian friends out there was Vette and I looked up to her. She had just one son, and she was a little older than me. Vette was living a holy life; didn't smoke, drink, or mess with men. She always invited us younger girls to church, but it wasn't our priority at the time because we were always busy doing something else. We respected her and our nonsense was never brought to her house. We didn't even talk like we would around her, out of respect. She would preach to us girls and tell us to do the right thing. I seems I heard God for the first time when I lived in Barberton; at a point when I was trying to sleep one night, He said, and I felt it, "knock at the door and seek and you shall find. I found out later that what He said was a part of a scripture.

Matthew 7:7 "Ask, and it shall be given you: Seek and ye shall find; knock and it will be opened to you." [KJV]

I was lonely, but I had several people surrounding me, I was searching, and didn't know what I was searching for. I think about what Solomon said in Ecclesiastes concerning 'Chasing the Wind' and it being futile, full of vanity and nothingness. I felt like screaming because nothing made me happy. Not these men, women, or the money satisfied me anymore. I was burnt out already at 19; tired of finding what I wasn't looking for...

Ecclesiastes 2:10 "And whatever my eyes desired I did not keep from them. I kept my heart from no pleasure." [ESV]

I started thinking about my purpose on this earth for real. I paged G-Money often, and most of the time he answered. I liked his company, and when we were together, I had no worries. He took me wherever I wanted to go. We spent a lot of time talking about everything; from G being raised by his grandmother to him growing up in Detroit and even going to catholic school. He was well rounded. Very articulate with his words and he kept my attention. I was attracted to him, but I kept it a secret even though it was mutual. I could feel it when we were together. Once G spent the night, and I was barely dressed lying next to him, he never touched me. I often wondered whether he was gay.

I kept this dude in the friend zone, and he told me everything; down to the woman he liked. G said he was attracted to bisexual women that was what he liked. We kissed once as he was dropping me off, the mood was just right, we were looking at each other and somebody leaned in, this wasn't an ordinary kiss. He made it special, and then he watched me walk in the house and then he pulled off. I think he purposely did that to make me want him more, but whatever game he was playing, I didn't want to play no more. I started throwing myself at him; giving him hints and my plan was to have sex with him, so I could get that control and upper hand over him, like most of us women know how to do.

Finally, it was official, and he took the lead, telling me everything he was going to do to me. I wasn't ready for him, and I wasn't controlling anything because he was in complete control. We began our thing, and many times I COULDN'T locate him. I had not seen G in about a week and had been paging him all day with no response. He had his disappearing acts when he would go to Detroit to see about his grandma or his kids, and he didn't owe me an explanation. I knew he was an "out in the streets dude" when I met him...

1st Peter 5:7...
"Casting all your anxieties on him, because he cares for you."
[ESV]

_____

_____

_____

_____

_____

_____

Pray this prayer:

Heavenly Father, as I read this book, turn my pressure and pain into the power of pain, allow it to change me, for my benefit and for the benefit of others ... by the power of your Holy Spirit. Allow forgiveness to flood my heart, change me for your purpose, and allow me to make a choice to use this pain for my benefit, and release it to You! Open my heart and mind to receive from You, allow me to heal from my past, allow me to move forward, and help others ...

... in Jesus' mighty name, Amen!

Chapter 10
"Going Deeper"

T he beginning of my fear of the Lord began when I read 2nd Samuel 24:13-16; when David took a census of Israel. Taking the census wasn't the sin, the reason behind it was. In the first verse, it said, "Satan stood against Israel and provoked King David to count his fighting men." That would display distrust in God, right? God did not tell David to number the troops' satan suggested it, but nevertheless, it was called sin and it kindled God's anger against Israel. David was given three choices of punishment for his sin: three years of famine, or three months of his enemies overtaking him or three days of the Sword of the Lord. David chose those three days of the sword of the Lord, reminding the Lord of His great mercy. But the Lord's punishment was so great as a result of that sin that 70,000 men lost their lives. David eventually cried out to God and said, "I am the one who called the census! I am the one who has sinned and done wrong! But these people are innocent like sheep-what have they done? O, Lord my God, let Your anger fall against me and my family, but do not destroy Your people!" David is described as a man after God's own heart, but even he couldn't escape God's punishment when it was necessary. I thought about my mistakes, and all that I had done. It became really clear that His mercy and grace was carrying me since I deserved His wrath. At that moment, my fear began. I paged G again, and this time I got a ring back, not from him but his sister; so, she claimed. She explained that he was locked up in the Summit County Jail, that he got caught up in a dope case, and she was just letting me know. It was short-lived, a matter of months because on his return, it seemed like he never left. When G came back into my life, he often took me out of town with him to places like Detroit. He was handling business, taking care of and seeing his family. I know he was getting his money back together after serving time in jail. He would take me to places I had never been. I was 19 but lied about my age, but just told him I didn't have my I.D so I still got in. We did talk about "his sister" who answered the phone, but I got even more confused when he told me that he didn't have a sister. He explained that they lived together though, and he came and went as he pleased, looked out for her but she wasn't his sister. Also, that they were sleeping together, but weren't actually together. I was young, and she was competition for me because he was supposed to be with me. We were an item; I and G, and I wasn't messing with anybody else. So, when he asked me if I want to have ménage trois with him and his fake sister, I was curious; curious about whom she was. Her name was Annette and she had three kids who were almost grown. She was nice though, and she kept a nice house, so I agreed, and we made a date for it. Days later it happened, I got to see G all the time and basically started staying with them. I would pack me an overnight bag and stay a week or so. Annette and G lived in Joy Park, Projects, in my old stomping grounds on the East Side of Akron. This situation with them was fun at first, but I started to get jealous. I began to desire G for myself, without Annette. I loved G and I felt, "why should I have to share him with anybody?" Nevertheless, he was the orchestrator of this thing with us.

G wanted this thing forever between us. I just wanted him, but I wanted to make him happy, and I know Annette did too. I knew I could do better than this. G told us both how much he loved us, and how much he enjoyed our family, and for a time, it was cool, but deep inside I felt stupid. Meanwhile, with my lack of staying in Barberton, my gas got cut off, and it was wintertime. It took me a few days to get the gas back on, and while it was out, it was cold in that apartment; so cold that the pipes burst. So, now I had to move, even though I had only stayed in Norton Homes a year and a few months. AMHA relocated me to the West Side, in Edgewood Apartments, 695 Westerly Rd. The apartment had been vacant for some years. My new neighbors let me know quickly about what had happened in my apartment before I moved there. I had family over here, some older cousins on my dad's side; Griffin's just like me. Other than family I didn't know anybody, hadn't lived on the Westside since my very beginning years.

Since I had moved here, I had not really dealt with G-Money. I was tired of sharing him. G was a street dude, he never really chilled around the house. Longing for someone of my own, he wanted this to be a permanent situation between us all. I ended up saying goodbye to our situation, after many fights and disagreements. I and G remained friends though.

It was exciting at first, making him happy and feeling good. G in the end did end up going to jail. They gave him five years, and we lost contact. Deep down inside, that need to be loved was deep inside, I was hurting, and I felt alone. It often brought me back to my childhood memories, and my ridiculous quest for love. I think I settled for that crazy relationship very strictly because I felt accepted, and in turn I accepted what came along with G. I barely had anybody. Mom really wasn't talking to me. My only steady support was my grandmother Ann and Aunt Renee (when she wasn't in prison). Also, I was basically alone with my kids throughout the day, besides when Jessica's grandmother had the girls.

Philippians 1:6, "I am convinced and confident of this very thing, that He who began a good work within you will [continue to] perfect and complete it until the day of Christ." [AMP]

I want you to meditate on this scripture! This one is really important. How many of you started off as the little girl with the ponytails sitting in Sunday School? How many of you had heard the Word of the Lord, and blatantly continued doing your own things? Seeds had been planted within you, each time you hear, because faith comes from hearing the Word of God. Sadly, such as the parable of the sower in Matthew 13:1-23, where Jesus explains, all seed does not fall on good soil, or good ground. Do you realize no one comes to God unless He is drawn? You didn't choose God. He chose you, and EVERYTHING YOU are. He chose you!

Ephesians 1:4, "For he chose us in him before the creation of the world to be holy and blameless in his sight." [NIV]

Regardless of mistakes and mishaps, and I know you know He knew you were going to mess up. God is not a quitter! He will complete those seeds within you and cause them to grow, to completion. He is faithful!

Psalms 86:11... "Teach me your way, O LORD; I will walk in Your truth; Unite my heart
to fear Your name." [NASB]

Pray this prayer:

Heavenly Father, ... as I read this book, turn my pressure and pain into the power of pain, allow it to change me, for my benefit and for the benefit of others ... by the power of your Holy Spirit. Allow forgiveness to flood my heart, change me for your purpose, and allow me to make a choice to use this pain for my benefit, and re-lease it to You! Open my heart and mind to receive from You, al-low me to heal from my past, allow me to move forward, and help others ...

...in Jesus' mighty name, Amen!

Chapter 11
"The Bloody Mary's"

E dgewood was only a temporary housing unit until A.M.H.A. came through with the decision that I was liable for the damages at my apartment where the pipes had burst in the winter. To be honest, I neglected to pay my gas bill, and it caused the damage, so I knew what the outcome was going to be. I started looking for other apartments outside of A.M.H.A. which were low income because if this didn't go in my favor, I would have to move. Rosemary Square/ Hillwood apartments were one of the places I was recommended to as I called around to different places applying for help. They went by your income and charged you a percentage of it. Most people like me [on welfare] were not required to pay rent, and we received a utility check to help pay the bills. It was in a place that of extreme convenience, close to everything for a single mother; The Arlington Plaza was in walking distance, which was the main attraction for the whole community. Taco Bell, Arby's and Wendy's were so close, you could send your child there and not feel guilty. I and Amber really got close, and we hung out a lot since she didn't have kids, and we were the exact same age. Amber went to college, lived in an apartment by herself and drove a new car just for graduating from high school. She was privileged, and her parents were rich, and they lived about 50 miles away in some suburb. You could never tell; Amber didn't grow up in the same environment as us because she was just as comfortable and hung out like the rest of us. We both bar-hopped and chased men and got high and fell for the dumb stuff and just had fun with these men and life. I met Amber in Edge-wood, when I lived there briefly.

We were 19 at the time, and Tupac's "All Eyes on Me" album had just come out that February. He was shot and killed 9-months later; September 7, 1996, at the age of 25. Tupac's death hit all of us literally; like he was our close friend. I still feel to this day that he was the greatest rapper alive. While I and Amber were slowly riding through Edgewood projects, bumping Tupac's "Check Out Time," a cute guy decided to stop right in front of us and start dancing to our music. I pulled over because he asked me to, and this wasn't the first time that I had seen him; he had fre-quented a neighbor in my building. It's not hard to figure out what somebody is doing if you watch them, and I paid attention. I had only been living there for three weeks and didn't really know anybody but my cousin, Wayne Griffin.

My cousin, stayed upstairs from me in one of those apartments with his "baby mama's" parents. This guy walked over to the car, and I quickly glanced at myself in the rearview mirror. He asked whether he could take me out at night, and I replied with a yes. What I didn't know was that this man had a career in prison be-fore he met me, and he was only 29. Joshua had served five years in a Federal Penitentiary for the transporting and use of drugs over state lines. When he got out of jail, he wanted to be on the other side of the deal, selling drugs, and not using them. Of course, we all know that it doesn't work all the time, and it's a temptation the majority can't handle. I met his mom within a couple of days, and she lived just a few streets over and owned a small corner store. I liked Shirley; She was cool, down to earth, and I could tell, Joshua was definitely a mama's boy. He was her oldest. He had three other siblings, and I could tell he dropped money over there on a regular. A lot came with the dope man,

I would find out, and it wasn't just the money or the good perks, but there also pain, other women, the drug dealer's lifestyle, the late-night hours, and the excessive traffic... in my house. Joshua also had a real job by day but was the "man at night" always carrying ounces on him at a time.

Joshua took care of me and my kids, kept me in nice clothes, my hair and nails stayed done. Joshua gave me money, gave me food stamps I never wanted for anything. That was the good stuff, but the bad was that I got into some drama with the other young girl he was messing with before me. When she found out that he had someone new, she got really mad and decided to come to my apartment with her friends. Guess whom one of them was? my friend Diana from Joy Park. The fight was called off. I and my girl stood in the street talking, while the other two just stood back and watched. At some point, I came home and there were two crack heads standing in my living room, but Joshua was nowhere in sight. I asked them where he was, and I was told he was in the backroom. I headed back there, but there was a strange look on their face. I made my way to the bedroom, and the door was closed. I knocked and tried to open it, but someone inside pushed the door back. I pushed harder, and it came open. To my surprise, behind the door was Joshua and a little skinny bald-headed dark-skinned crack head on her knees. Her mutter of I'm sorry did not stop me from hitting her and him too with the 40 oz bottle that was sitting nearby. By the end of that night, he was laying right next to me, claiming he loved me, though he messed up. I wasn't even listening, instead, I was patiently waiting for him to go to sleep so I could hit his pockets and make him pay for playing me.

Then there was the time I left Amber there to give somebody a ride, but she was drunk. I came back to find out that Joshua had slept with my friend; she claimed she was drunk, and that he came onto her. I got mad and so focused on getting his money, that I didn't even care. I was cold-hearted and couldn't afford to care.

I forgave her and myself too, and me and Amber remained friends.

I moved out within two weeks, after I stayed in Edgewood about four months, and one of my first letters at my new address was from A.M.H.A., telling me they made their decision. I lost my subsidy, and I needed to move out within 30 days. I was already gone, so this was irrelevant to me. Joshua moved in with me, and shortly after I moved to the Hillwood Apartments, I found out I was pregnant for the third time (six-weeks pregnant). A few weeks after we moved in, Joshua got his parole revoked at six weeks of my pregnancy, but when he got out of jail, my 3rd daughter Desiree was already eight months old. I was 21 with three daughters and no husband, but when Joshua got out of jail, we got married.

It was at the courthouse, and we had planned a very big reception, though we never had it. Two weeks after we married, my sister came over to tell me that Joshua had come to her house, and that he had come on to her to beg her for money, and that made me so mad. My sister! Considering what Joshua had already put me through, I was tired and decided to end our relationship and put him out. Back when we lived in Edgewood, I went to the hospital one night because I suddenly broke out in hives. They never did find out what I was allergic to but gave me some Benadryl and sent me home. When I arrived home, Joshua was there, and I noticed a crack head and incenses burning in the corner. I asked why, and he said nothing but grabbed his bag and muttered something about making a move. I found out later the next day when he came back that he had relapsed. We sat and talked about his past, and he told me how he used to live in California back when crack first emerged back in '86. He tried crack and liked it, but this was before the consequences were told, and also before the crack epidemic began. Joshua promised me that it was an isolated incident, and he wasn't going to do it anymore, and that he was back on track. That wasn't the last time though, and that was the very reason he went back to jail and went over my sister's house with that nonsense.

I was tired, as a young woman and I felt that I should not have to do all the extra stuff to be satisfied and happy, and to keep a man. Since he was my husband, I felt that's what I had to do though. I had put myself in harm's way many, many times because of his drug abuse, and nothing worked. As the years went by in the Rosemary projects, I learned what project life was about, and I slowly and surely became a product of my environment. I did what project chic's do. I lived a life loyal to the projects, and to my newfound family in the hood. I learned how to sell drugs back in Edgewood, and after Joshua's initial relapse. I learned very quickly that crack can bring you down to absolutely nothing. In the end, when I met Joshua, he had nothing and would steal from a change jar we used for emergencies. I literally watched him go down from a big-time dope dealer to a crack head in a matter of months. He went down to a monotonous lifestyle, even to one mission only. That was to get high, regardless of the pain it caused his family. He continued full throttle and could barely hold down a job. Every week I had to be right there with him to cash his checks and to get the money from him ever before he could mess up with it. I would go to the extreme to get his money from him, even catching a cab to his job, to take him to cash his check every week. He would hop in the cab and be gone on his mission. When he got tired of being in the crack houses, and when it was time to go to work, he would ask me whether he could come home. Out of love and pity, I would let him come back home to shower, shave, and eat and lay in the bed with me. I started viewing him as a weak childish, incompetent man, but my view of all men was really like that. I didn't respect men, and I knew in my heart they would soon leave and be unreliable. It's also in some way how I felt about my dad. He left me, didn't keep his promise to me, and now he was gone and never to return. I don't know if I loved Joshua, but that wasn't what I was driven by, and not even my purpose for getting married. It just seemed to be the right thing to do, living and working it out with your baby daddy, on the behalf of your child. I was unhappy though. Meanwhile, life in the hood was good; I had met a group of guys up there, and I started hanging with them. It started off as a come by hang out and smoke, but over the years, I stayed up there. It became much more because the members consisted of the East Side of Akron, or they were affiliated with them. They all wore red, and most of them rapped, made music, sold drugs, had guns, ran the projects, and most people were scared of them. Their reputation of intimidation was to those who were not from around that area, but otherwise, you were cool. They were strict when it came to the color or the gang affiliation, or anything past 5th avenue off of Arlington St., all the way through 1st avenue, Joy Park, streets like Chittenden and Lover's Lane. I was what you called a big sister to them, though we were all of the same age. A few of them were older than me though. Although I was never formally initiated, I was given the name Big Mama Compton which eventually got shortened down to just Compton. I was known for fighting and selling drugs, and not somebody you want to mess with; I became my "brother's safe haven." A place where they could always turn for whatever, and in turn, they became my brothers. They looked out for me, watched over me, and they even helped out with the kids.

When Desiree was young, I had a rocking chair, and they used to rock her in it. They would have me make a grocery list and they would buy the food. They would buy breakfast and I would cook, and we would have big barbeques. They would cook all the meat on the grill, and I would make all the side dishes. The kids would be outside playing, music blasted, but we had fun. They would get jealous if I wanted a boyfriend, and he would have to be able to stand up to them. My brothers had expectations of me and wanted me to date inside of the group. I had dealings with a couple of them. They were hood relationships, but it was never serious and most of them never worked out.

Because of some fire that my neighbor started in the building when I stayed at 1105 Tarson Terrace in 1998 we had to move overnight because of smoke damage. I was glad to go from that apartment honestly because I went to jail behind one of my neighbors. I was walking to my door one day and she stopped me, telling me about my husband; that he tried to talk to her and offered her oral sex. I checked with Joshua and of course, he lied. Over the next few days, this girl kept talking recklessly to me. She had her door opened wide one day, and I ran in there to beat her up. We tore her place up fighting. I spit on Joshua in front of the police, for getting me in this mess in the first place. I was arrested for Assault Misdemeanor-1 and Domestic Violence, so I didn't spend any time in jail. They wasted their time riding me down there because Summit County Jail was full. This was my first time going to jail as an adult, so I was sent back home, deemed low risk.

I and my mom were up and down, but I and my sister had over the years got so close. She recently had her 3rd baby; a son, by one of my "hood brothers" whom she was messing around with. She never let his dad get into his life; never let him see her baby and was trying to give him up for adoption and had made plans to do so until I talked to her and made her come stay with me. I wanted to help her with the baby, so she wouldn't feel overwhelmed. After staying about a week with me, she ended up keeping the baby.

I thought back then that I was a good mother, but from my view years later, I admitted I wasn't. The things I exposed them to, and the things I did. My mentality back then was I'd rather be in jail if I couldn't provide for them like I wanted to.

My mother's health had dwindled down over the years, and Andrea had become her right-hand man. It started when she started having complications due to her diabetes, and she was diagnosed with congestive heart failure. She had a heart attack and had to have an open-heart surgery; none of which I was there. She didn't let me be, but mostly because I didn't want to be. I felt out of place, and not a part of them. I just stayed away eventually.

Andrea went to jail for passing bad checks, which was a felony five, so I obtained her two kids. Andrea and Nightmare had opened bank accounts and deposited fake checks. She had got a letter in the mail stating the money had cleared, and she could pick up her money. Her and Nightmare, my hood brother, had got three hundred from the ATM when the account first opened up. Andrea asked me to ride with her that day when she went to pick it up. She went into the bank and never came out until the police pulled up behind me, and on to the driver's side window to tell me I had to get out of the car. They also demanded me to surrender my niece and nephew to C.S.B. because she was going to jail. Then I see my sister being led out of the bank in handcuffs; I gave the police offi-cers a hard time and wouldn't open the window or door until my sister finally gave consent for me to keep the kids. We hopped on a bus after we walked what seemed like a mile because I was deter-mined to be my sister's keeper and to keep her kids.

I now had three children by this time, and I was working odd jobs through a temp service called Minute Man when I could get a regular babysitter. I usually had no help unless I knew someone from the hood, since we all looked out for each other if we weren't fighting over a man and such. Drama was the usual lifestyle of the projects, but you could avoid it if you minded your own business and stayed to yourself. That was hard to do, considering people were broke and had nothing to do. At almost 23-years-old, I was getting tired of this project life. I had worked at a few fast-food restaurants like Arby's and Taco Bell around the hood within walking distance. The temporary agency across the street sent me to plastic factories, and none of them did I enjoy. I had thought about the medical field because I liked helping people.

I began mingling and meeting my new neighbors. Lesha lived across the hall from my place, but on the bottom floor, and her mother lived with her. She was an older lady and seemed to be watching her grandchild throughout the day. I would see Ma Dukes sitting on our community porch, sitting in a chair, smoking on a cigarette, reading the newspaper. We had small talk, would smoke a cigarette together, then we would part ways, and continue about our day. One morning, I set out to ask her a question because something about her felt motherly. I had to ask Ma Dukes if she babysits kids. Ma Dukes started babysitting my kids, and I paid her good money. She became more of a nanny. Not only was she babysitting, but she was cleaning my house. She was doing homework with the kids, cooking, and driving my kids to and from where they had to go while I worked. She was even much more than that. Ma Dukes was gay and acted like a man. She was 36 years old, but when I asked her to babysit that day, she offered much more than just babysitting. We started this down-low relationship, and it lasted roughly seven years. We even thought about getting married. It wasn't legal after all. She took care of my kids, she was there to meet my mother, and was introduced as my friend though I loved her beyond friendship. That was our problem actually, she wanted a public relationship, and I wasn't having it. I wasn't gay, but this was an opportunity that benefitted both of us. I got pregnant again with technically my 5th child, while we were still in a relationship. I had a miscarriage by Joshua a few years before that, but she still stuck by me and was at the delivery room when I had him. Desmond, my first son was born on January 2004, 9 pounds, 3 ounces and 21 inches long. A few months later, I decided to look for a house and get out of those projects. One night I made seven hundred in one-night selling drugs, and I was able to move I and my kids out of those projects in less than a week, to the North Side of Akron. Now, it was April of 2004.

Psalms 139:7-8...

"Where can I go from your Spirit? Or where shall I flee from Your presence? If I ascend to heaven, you are there! if I make my bed in Sheol, you are there!" [ESV]

_____

_____

_____

_____

_____

_____

Pray this prayer along with me:

Heavenly Father, ...as I read this book, turn my pressure and pain into the power of pain, allow it to change me, for my benefit and for the benefit of others ...by the power of your Holy Spirit. Allow forgiveness to flood my heart, change me for your purpose, and allow me to make a choice to use this pain for my benefit, and release it to You! Open my heart and mind to receive from You, allow me to heal from my past, and allow me to move forward, and help others too...

... in Jesus' mighty name, Amen!

Chapter 12
"Revelation Pt. 1"

I had lived in the projects for a total of eight years, and it was past time for me to go. I wasn't running from anything or anybody, but more like running to a new future. I didn't know what that consisted of, I just kept thinking bigger and better for me, and my children. I left because I was tired and had enough of the life I was living in those projects. I was 27 now, and with what life had to offer, I was burnt out; I had experienced it all. I reflected often on my past and started hating myself for my past mistakes. At one point I even contemplated suicide but didn't have the nerve to do it. In my mind I had failed as a parent, as a person, and as a human being, and God was nowhere around.

How could He care for me when He had allowed me to go through this pain? I couldn't see it then, but as I got older and more matured, I started seeing things in a whole new light. Instead of blaming God for my mistakes, I started blaming myself. I was selfish while the whole time I was claiming to love others, including my children. I was searching for something but didn't quite know what it was, because at this point, all I knew was pain. I was angry, hurt, feeling justified for some of the things I had done, and for the other things I just did out of pure anger. When it came to my children, I "told" myself I was a good mother because I did everything in the world materially for them, but I wasn't physically and affectionately there for them.

I would often leave my kids at home by themselves, and I didn't think anything was wrong with that. My mom used to leave me and Andrea home alone when I was seven, while she worked. What I didn't realize was that I was repeating the same with my children. The same things I said about my mother, my children were saying about me. I didn't nurture them, and I hardly spent time with them. Since Jessica was the oldest, I put most of my responsibility on her. Jessica was thirteen, Monica was ten, Desiree' was seven, and Desmond was four-months-old. When I moved to the North Side, and I was 27, my kids had grown up with me, and I was more of a friend than a parent to them. I started having problems with Jessica's mouth, and Monica was having problems in school. I had my own battle with a disease that I was diagnosed of having in 1999, Multiple Sclerosis. Although I was walking, working, and living my life, I wouldn't take my medication regularly, and I didn't tell anybody I had it. I didn't know what to think, and my life became uncertain because of what I did know. What I didn't know about this disease was the onset of it, and the symptoms it brought made me nervous. It was what could happen that haunted me. I had several patients as a home health aide with M.S., and none of them were doing good.

Ma Dukes and I fought constantly. Our relationship was not all good, and in 1999 I stabbed Ma Dukes twice when she came after me at my house carrying a baseball bat. This all happened during my last months in the projects. I was looking at eight years for Felonious Assault, and as I sat in the Summit County Jail for two days, they finally let me out on a signature bond. When I got out, my kids were in the custody of C.S.B., but when I left, they were with my mom and sister. Nobody had an explanation as to why they were there, but when I got out, I had to get them back. I and Ma Dukes formed a plan, and she wrote a lengthy letter to the judge explaining everything to be her fault. The charges were dropped, and I got my kids back. As I look back now on my life and on others who chose this lifestyle; in fact, I have very rarely seen a homosexual relationship work i.e., Being happy and not having a relationship of jealousy, strife, cheating, or a whole lot of mess. The reason is that relationships not ordained by God do not have His covering or protection. They lack Him being in the midst. I was browsing the internet and found a blog on "How to discern if you are in a God-ordained relationship," written by Taylor on July 22, 2015. It is not just limited to homosexual relationships, but to all relationships. I could not find the blog again and I wanted to give this woman proper credit for her work, since her article changed my life.

Taylor wrote: "In thinking about my last relationship, there was nothing wrong with my ex as a person. In fact, the sudden ending to the relationship surprised many people. The public break-up was only a manifestation of a private process I had been experiencing for a couple of months. In 2008-2009, I began to draw closer to God and to thirst for His word like never before. While my ex was a member of my local church, he was not ready to make a full commitment to Christ. It would be unfair for me to expect or require something of someone who was not ready. I truly believe that each of us has our own stories and God deals with us differently. However, it was CLEAR that God was dealing with me THEN. I realized I had never consulted God about the relationship; better late than never and still 2 years late. So, in consulting God, I found that the relationship was NOT God ordained and that it had to be ended (this was not as easy for me to do as it is for you to read). To ordain is to enact or enable by law; to confer holy orders upon or to destine or predestine. In other words, God ordained relationships are relationships that God himself approves of. This is not restricted to spousal relationships but extends to all relationships with friends, mentors, church leaders etc. We serve a God who cares about every facet of our lives and carefully plans our lives down to the very hairs on our body (Mt

10:30). Given His attention to detail, I believe he deeply cares about whom we choose to spend our time with. The people we surround ourselves with should always push us closer to Christ. For me not to consult with God before entering my last relationship was WRONG. When we as believers tell God that we submit to HIS will and HIS way, we cannot leave out our dating lives or friendships. I have decided to relinquish control of ALL my relationships. If God does not approve of any of my relationships, then they simply must END Point Blank, Period. It is never easy to accept the instruction to end a relationship, but I also do not want to know the consequences of not obeying God's instructions." End of Taylor's blog.

1st Samuel 15:23, "For rebellion is as the sin of witchcraft, and stubbornness is as idolatry and teraphim. Because thou hast rejected the word of the LORD, He hath also rejected thee from being king.' [JPS]

1st John 3:4-10, "Everyone who practices sin also practices lawlessness; and sin is lawlessness [ignoring God's law by action or neglect or by tolerating wrongdoing—being unrestrained by His commands and His will]. You know that He appeared [in visible form as a man] to take away sins; and in Him there is [absolutely] no sin [for He has neither the sin nature nor has He committed sin or acts worthy of blame]. No one who abides in Him [who remains united in fellowship with Him—deliberately, knowingly, and habitually] practices sin. No one who habitually sins have seen Him or known Him. 7 Little children (believers, dear ones) do not let anyone lead you astray. The one who practices righteousness [the one who strives to live a consistently honorable life —in private as well as in public—and to conform to God's precepts] is righteous, just as He is righteous. The one who practices sin [separating himself from God, and offending Him by acts of disobedience, indifference, or rebellion] is of the devil [and takes his inner character and moral values from him, not God]; for the devil has sinned and violated God's law from the beginning. The Son of God appeared for this purpose, to destroy the works of the devil. No one who is born of God [deliberately, knowingly, and habitually] practices sin, because God's seed [His principle of life, the essence of His righteous character] remains [permanently] in him [who is born again—who is reborn from above—spiritually transformed, renewed, and set apart for His purpose]; and he [who is born again] cannot habitually [live a life characterized by] sin, because he is born of God and longs to please Him. By this the children of God and the children of the devil are clearly identified: anyone who does not practice righteousness [who does not seek God's will in thought, action, and purpose] is not of God, nor is the one who does not [unselfishly] love his [believing] brother." [AMP]

James 1:15, "Then, after desire has conceived, it gives birth to sin; and sin, when it is full-grown, gives birth to death."[NIV]

Although sin feels good to our nature, and often feels natural, but then it brings forth death and its very nature comes from within us still. Sin was attached to our very nature at birth and became our birthright. Once we took that first step into sin, we agreed with our nature. Now, how many people can look back and remember their first sin? The first time you lied, the first time you stole, probably nobody, and I can bet it happened as a child when you were innocent and guess what, no one taught you to sin. Small opportunities came up along the way, pitfalls and such, to make sin readily available and easier to fall deeper in. Once you do something more than once, twice or a few times, even if you don't totally like it, it becomes a habit (something you're used to doing). I have heard that even harmful, hurtful things can become a habit, especially when it raises certain feelings and emotions related to sin. Homosexuality is just one of man's rebellions against God. By that, I'm not trying to say that such persons are above God, or that my way is better. Such persons are actually saying God's plan is not good enough for them, and that they can do better. If God intended for us to be gay, why then does the Holy Bible say that we won't inherit the kingdom of God with such life. Most of us would complain that it doesn't apply to us, but if one practices lawlessness [continuing in sin, with no regard to consequences,] it actually refers to such person!

1st Corinthians 6:9-10, "Or do you not know that wrongdoers will not inherit the kingdom of God? Do not be deceived: Neither the sexually immoral nor idolaters nor adulterers nor men who have sex with men nor thieves nor the greedy nor drunkards nor slanderers nor swindlers will inherit the kingdom of God." [NIV]

We all need to be justified for our actions, and that makes us feel decent on the inside. No matter how I tried to justify my actions, I'm here to tell you I still felt convicted of my sin! This was before I knew and understood what convictions were. I tried to ignore them, but I never felt "totally comfortable" in my sin. God gives us free will, and for most of us, we exercised that right and did everything that came to our minds, against God; Just because we felt like it or felt like we were wronged and felt like we deserved it. This wasn't my last homosexual experience, but it was the most important or significant one. Until I got serious enough about coming into agreement with God's word and wanting to please Him above myself, did I change.

Deliverance is available if you want it, but you must want it. Look at it as a disobedient child. You love them, and because you love them, after a while, if it is in your power you talk to them first, then take things away next. If that doesn't correct the behavior, more serious consequences follow. It starts with the recognition of your wrong, putting your life in the hands of someone greater, trusting in His plans for your life, and stepping out on faith to change. Regardless of your circumstances and why you came to be this way, most of you believe you were born that way, and that is a lie. Although you may not be able to pinpoint the day or hour you came into agreement with that spirit, you did. Some of us were born with the spirit of sin attached to us from our ancestors, some 3rd and 4th generations before us.

When we pondered and acted on it, we came into agreement with it. Opportunities are provided for the sin that we lack in our own lives. Think about it, if you need money, an opportunity will arise for you to steal. Now, if we lack love, a counterfeit one will be provided. And, if we've been rejected, acceptance will come but with a price (Psalms 103:1-12). Notice the offer always comes before the Promise, as in Abraham and Ishmael versus Isaac the promise. It's a shame I was willing to pay that price called sin to be happy, many times. I disregarded the truth for my truth, and the conflict was internal because the truth was deep within me. I knew the truth, but I wasn't trying to hear and follow it since I wasn't happy, and above all I didn't feel approved by God. I made it up in my mind that He hated me because of my life's unnecessary pain. Even though I was the cause of my present predicament, it was Him I felt was responsible for my "family issues" and the cause of the madness I put myself through. Back around the Rosemary's, I started going to a church named 'In HIS light.' The church was small with just a few faithful members; a few young women, single mothers just like me. The Pastor was an attractive young man; short with a Jerri Curl in his early 40's and was unmarried with no children. The "First Lady" of the church was also the mother of the church, and she always spoke much wisdom to us, young girls. Mother Brady always spoke in a stern way, letting us know that we had boundaries in our conversations with her. We respected her. Mother Brady was an older lady in her 70's with grey hair, and I looked up to her. When she talked, I listened because she had a mouth full of wisdom. Mother Brady reminded me of my grandmother Ann because when older people would talk, I learned to listen; they were not talking for their health, they would often say to me. Then there was Ms. Minnie who considered herself as the Prophetess of the house. Meanwhile, in my new home and new environment, I had a new job, met a few new friends in my neighborhood. I met Mona, a Mexican-Indian lady who lives a few doors down from me and Desiree', my youngest daughter. Desiree' always wanted to go to her friends' house, so I had to go and see whom this friend was, as well as her mother. As soon as I and Mona met, we became the best of friends. I also met the man who lived across the street from me. His name was Tony, and he was 43. I had just turned 28 at the time. Tony was nice looking for an older man. I was bored lonely and single and new to the area too. He liked keeping me company, and it was never about sex. He kept me company; we watched movies and spent a lot of time together. It wasn't long before our relationship changed, and he was living with me. I was expecting my fifth child.

While I was still attending In HIS light in 2005, I met Ms. Minnie, the Prophetess aged between 35-37 years old. Nice young and hip, with a lot of wisdom. She latched on to us young girls in the church, talking about her past life with men and drugs. She put us together for a singing group, and she was kind of hard on us, forcing us to sing when we didn't even want to, even embarrassing us. She couldn't sing a lick, but we could. We heard rumors that she was in love with the pastor. The pastor had never been married before; no wife, no girlfriend, and I heard he wasn't dating. He had a mansion, liked nice things, and had many cars; he actually invited us to his mansion, for the church's Christmas party. Ms. Minnie, as it was told to us, put herself on the pulpit, and we heard she wasn't ordained as a Prophet. She obviously had a gift prophesying over us girls all the time, telling us what 'Thus sayeth the Lord.' She always told me I could see if I look under the right light. I never understood that. I was on the phone with Ms. Minnie one day the day Holy Spirit came to me (the day it manifested). I had the chills all day, feeling very weird. I called her seeking help, but then I don't know why somehow, I just knew it was God, since I had been seeking Him deeply. I was still hurt from the past and searching for a way to relieve the pain. I was smoking daily, and my child's father was living with me. I was lonely but not alone. I was working in the factory for a steel company through a temp agency, but I was making it happen. On the day of the chills, I thought my M.S. was acting up, especially since I had only been diagnosed for a few years. I actually didn't know what to expect. I stammered the first words of my heavenly language and cried out to the Lord in that language I did not know. As I spoke, she spoke what I said, "I Was a Daughter of The King, He did love me, I was oppressed because of my destiny, I had the gift of discernment, the gift of healing, and I was special to God Almighty." I walked in that same anointing for a couple of years after that. Being woke up at night, with Him speaking to me as I was getting back to bed, "I'm preparing you for something big." I wondered what He meant by that. I'd be on the job with supernatural strength, not even feeling tired because I didn't get any rest the night before; up reading the word, praying and listening to Him speak. He gave me visions and many dreams; some I understood and some I didn't. I knew His voice now, and that I was trying to follow. I went to church faithfully, took my kids and got really involved in the choir.

My boyfriend still lived with me he was 14-years older senior whom I planned to marry. Jonathan our son was born precisely 2 years after my oldest son Desmond. I dreamt one day of how the Lord said I would have 3 kings and 3 queens. That meant one more child, a boy, I would have.

Galatians 3:5 ...

"He therefore that gives unto you the Spirit and does works of power among you, does he do it by the works of the law or by the obedient ear of faith?"

[JUB]

Pray this prayer:

Heavenly Father, ...as I read this book, turn my pressure and pain into the power of pain, allow it to change me, for my benefit and for the benefit of others ...by the power of your Holy Spirit. Allow forgiveness to flood my heart, change me for your purpose, and allow me to choose to use this pain for my benefit, and release it to You! Open my heart and mind to receive from You, allow me to heal from my past, allow me to move forward, and help others...

... in Jesus' mighty name, Amen

Chapter 13
"The Revelation Pt 2"

Since 2004, I had moved three times and this was the third house I had been in on the North Side, on Blaine and Tallmadge Rd. The first house I moved into from the projects was on Dayton St, it had roaches and was ragged; I ended up moving within a year. Next, I found a 4-bedroom house where we ended up settling in for about six years on Chalker St. I and Tony were still together raising my kids and our son together. Shortly after we moved in together, I found out the raw truth. Tony was married and he was a serious alcoholic. He didn't drink constantly but when he did, it was horrible. He wasn't violent, and we didn't fight, but his mouth and his behavior were terrible. Tony's wife Alexandria was an older lady, and a bitter one at that. From the moment she found out about me, we had a problem.

Jonathan was Tony's first child and out of him and Alexandria's twenty something years of marriage, they had no children together. She did have one biological one though, and because I had my son by Tony, she hated me. Tony's brother lived directly across the street from me on Dayton St. which was how we met. Tony just got up and left home one day and Alexandria had got up and left too, taking a trip with her friend and without Tony. Tony dropped her off at the airport and then came back to their house, packed his clothes and moved over to his brother's house. I guess he felt some type of way about her going on the trip without him, and they were already having problems. By the time she returned home, she had no understanding why he was gone.

When she got back from that vacation, she realized that he was gone and had not returned because of me. She came by a few times to let me know when he was cheating and eventually filed for a divorce. Alexandria thrived on drama. At one time we would talk on the phone so much she asked me to come over and sleep with her, but I never did. I wasn't a cheater, though the things Tony put me through made me wander. During those times between 2005-2009, I worked many jobs. 3rd shift jobs doing home health aide work, factory jobs, and temporary assignments. If we weren't both working together the other one stayed home with the kids. Tony was older and when it came to my daughters, I would rarely let him say anything to them. My daughters never liked him, and they barely respected him, but he was the only father Desmond knew.

Colin was Desmond's real father, and a product of a few nights of a love affair. Me and Colin never pursued a relationship, and we knew each other from high school and just happened to link up. Colin had many other children and was living with a woman at the time and driving her car when we ran into each other again. When I found out I was pregnant, he told me to go get an abortion and he offered no support.

Tony was a terrible father to my kids and his son. He provided well financially and that was only a few times. Other than that, Tony was never there.

We couldn't stand him because he was always drunk and disrespectful to me, and he called us names. Jessica told me he was way too close when he drank, and I paid attention, but I felt he was just old and drunk. I never felt there was any need to worry, black men don't mess with children, so I thought. It came as a complete shock when one-night, Monica had spent the night with a friend of hers, and they were having a super bowl party, and there was a blizzard so bad that we couldn't go back and get her. Tony and I dropped her off and gave her a couple of dollars for her pocket. The next day we picked her up, and as we were riding home, I asked Monica whether she did spend her money. She said that it came up missing and she doesn't know where it went. As a parent, that really concerned me, so as Monica got ready for me to drop her off at school, I knew when I got back home that I was going to be making it my business to call Charmaine, the boy's mother to see how she was doing, and find out about my child's money. Later on, I and Charmaine talked. Caught up from the last time I saw her, we discussed our old mutual friends then I asked about Monica's money. What Charmaine said next floored me. She said that she did catch her son, and my daughter in the shower together. Charmaine explained to them both that it was inappropriate. Next, she said they had a private conversation, and she talked to my daughter about being a young lady. Monica confided in Charmaine that Tony had been touching and messing with her. I was in complete shock. Meanwhile, Tony had been listening to the whole time; he denied it and I didn't believe it either. When Monica got out of school, I questioned her, and she denied it. I was puzzled, though I eventually let it go. Why would Charmaine lie? She didn't even know my boyfriend's name.

Since I had been diagnosed with Multiple Sclerosis in 1999, I had limited issues. If you looked at me on the outside, I looked normal just like anybody else. I got headaches sometimes, had numb fingers, and walked like my equal Librium was off. Most of my symptoms had gone away due to the diagnosis and the medication. The other symptoms, you won't see them. I had to give myself a shot; subcutaneously daily. Copaxone was the drug they chose and so far, it was doing its job when I decided to take it. I did not take it as prescribed, as I forgot, or simply because I just didn't want to. I suffered for my poor choices when years later

I started having issues with walking. While I was walking, my legs would often fail me. In 2006 it began to be noticeable to others. When I would walk, I would lean up against people and Tony got me a cane that I could use. Tony told me often that nobody would want me in my condition and that I needed him in case it got worse. Besides him, I didn't have anybody. Even my mom and sister were on and off.

Andrea lived a few streets away from me. She had wild parties on weekends and made it her business to be in church on Sunday Morning. I commended her for being able to pull that off because I know I couldn't. Meanwhile, my mother was going to a Mormon church; she had left her apostolic church home. I started going to a Pentecostal church around the corner, after I left 'In His light,' as I moved over to the North side. I still hung out with Sis. Minnie a lot, and she became my soul confidant and she eventually told me that I was her spiritual daughter. I looked up to her but looking back I was actually seduced by prophecy; her words were soothing.

Ms. Minnie spoke into my life so often; I started looking and longing for the things she said. Ms. Minnie was holding webcasts online and having regular prayer meetings at her house. I was always there and others at the church would come but not many. We would sing songs, read the Bible and she would preach, teach and prophesy. She was always the one in control. She eventually quit coming to church altogether. After the baptism of the Holy Spirit came upon me in 2005, my life had never been the same. I knew things, I had visions, and He talked so much to me. It was so hard to contain it. I read the Bible like a maniac. Every waking moment, I wanted to sit in His presence. I wanted to hear His voice, and I wanted to learn.

In 2005 I didn't know at the time what the gift of healing and discernment was, but I made it my business to search the web and find everything I could on those subjects and the gifts of GOD

(Gifts of the Holy Spirit). I found out that there are nine of them. *The Word of Wisdom, The Word of Knowledge, Faith, Miracles, Prophecy the Discernment of Spirits, Tongues, Interpretation of Tongues* and *Healing.* What I read satisfied my curiosity but did not satisfy my spirit, although it did prepare me for what was to come. When I heard prophecies spoken, I could tell if it were accurate because it would give me such a peace if it was right.

I sat in prophet's meetings and had friends who prophesied, but I would never tell anyone about what I personally saw and heard; I just kept it to myself. I didn't have anyone to talk to about what was going on within me. I felt as if nobody would understand my personal situation. Ms. Minnie had a Prayer meeting at Mother Brady's house one day, and she invited me. I invited a friend of mine, Prophetess Daisy Nance. When I asked her to come with me, she replied that God had told her that she needed to go somewhere, so she immediately accepted. I had met other women who prophesied and for some reason, I was drawn to that. Growing up in an apostolic church I had seen many things, so I was no stranger to seeing the Holy Spirit move.

Now I speak in tongues, and when I speak, a whole other conversation would be going on in my head. I did talk to Sister Minnie about me speaking in tongues before, and she told me I had a lot of gifts. Honestly, when I hear people speak, it's almost like their conversation slowed down for me to hear. I heard His voice often after that, and I felt things, but I still didn't understand what she meant.

I drove to the meeting by myself, and my friend said she would meet me there, Daisy was an ordained Prophet at her church and was a well-respected woman. When I got there, there were four people whom I didn't know. Ms. Minnie was among them. They greeted me as I sat down and watched and noticed it didn't seem structured, but more of a relaxed atmosphere. My friend came shortly after that with her Armor bearer, her husband and their child. They sat down, and when they introduced themselves, they let it be known that I was the one who invited them. Daisy asked if she could release a word that she had for someone in the group. She was given permission and when she was giving the release, she began to pray for one of the women. When she got done praying for her, Daisy was on her way to pray for someone else in the room and before she could, Sis Minnie asked her to stop. I was in awe as I watched the Armor bearer stopped Sis Minnie, and all of this became an issue, so my friend Daisy left. They argued with Sis. Minnie for a minute before they were told that they were not welcome, and they took their exit. I was embarrassed, but more than that I saw and felt something in Ms. Minnie that I had never seen before. It became very apparent to me, that the wool over my eyes was lifted. The Lord God started reading those spirits off to me, *vanity*, and the spirit of *manipulation*. I didn't know what to say. I respected and loved Ms. Minnie, and this was all new to me. I felt Ms. Minnie was wrong; why would she stop a move of God when we're doing nothing but singing songs? I had so many questions about what happened, but none of them ever got answered because she cut me off. I ran into her a couple of times after that and at random places, and when I would call her, she would give me the cold shoulder. The last time I saw her, I was parked at a gas pump. I looked up and saw her coming out of the store into the parking lot. I turned back around, and she was at my car door. We had a small talk and then she walked away. A few months later, I heard she was found dead in her home at the age of 51. I was completely at a loss when I heard that. I loved that woman like a mother! I found out later she still used cocaine and that may have been the cause of her death, though they just said her heart gave out.

Things between I and Tony were not good, but our relationship wasn't traditional. We both had our mess ups in the relationship. I would often wake up at night and he wouldn't be lying next to me. I did love him, but we had more of a relationship of convenience. I gave him something he wanted, a son but his heart was still with Alexandria, his ex-wife. He still shared himself with her emotionally and he didn't with me. He would cheat on her with me, and he would cheat on me with her, but I cheated too in paying him back for hurting me. I got caught a few times. Once in Cleveland, Tony was fixing houses with his brother. I drove all the way to Cleveland to meet this dude, and along for the ride was my girl, Diana. We arrived at his house and decided to go out to the club. The guy I met up with, had a friend for Diana, but she didn't like his friend. We were drunk as we left and headed over to my new friends' house. Diana wanted to meet up with a guy she met from the club and wanted to use my car. I let her, and this was four (4) a.m. Dianna never came back. She got arrested and my car got towed. I was stranded in Cleveland, with my kids at home. I had a headache by this point and blamed everything on Diana. I kept my mouth shut and called Tony. He paid the money towards my tow and cussed me out. Another time, one of my friends whom I was caught with was also my girlfriend Mona's brother-in-law. He was my friend, my boyfriend on the side, and a steady shoulder to cry on. That night, because I was bold, and I figured Tony would be drunk and pass out, I was planning to go to Will's house later. Will had been traveling with us that night, posing as my girl Diana's boyfriend the whole night. I decided to pick him up, to keep my girl company, and because I personally wanted to be with and around him. The night ended horribly, with me catching Tony get into the car with his ex-wife and me chasing them in my car.

It was more about my children and what I wanted when it came to Tony. Although we stayed together, I started seeking friends and other relationships because deep inside, I really wanted to leave him. We had a child together, and Tony, unlike the rest of my children's dads did stick around. His son grew up knowing his father and woke up to him every day of his life until the age of six. I must be honest, that was the glue that kept us together. I didn't see a future with Tony anymore, so he was viewed as an outsider. A threat to me, and my children's happiness. Church and God had become a necessity, through it all since God had revealed Himself to me. One night as I was preparing to go to bed, God spoke to me; "*I am preparing you for something big.*" I had searched for Him. Deep in my heart I needed Him! Change began in me.

I quit smoking weed, started changing my thinking, and stopped being so mean to people. It was like God softened my heart. I still had bitterness and unforgiveness in my heart but something within me changed for the better. I was naturally mean, and because I had been mean for so long, I honestly didn't know any other way to be. I had to look back on my life and take a really hard look at myself.

The night at the gas station with Will, after our night of drinking; out of nowhere, I saw Tony walking through the parking lot, staggering and talking to himself. I lost my train of thought and forgot I was with Will. I opened my car door and yelled at Tony, but he kept on walking. He kept walking along the street, and just like that I saw Alexandria's car pull up, and he hopped in. I stood there in awe as they pulled off, but it didn't take long for me to react. I hopped in my car and chased them. I had forgotten that Will was in the car and had just seen red. Around the corner from the gas station was St. Thomas hospital, and that's where Alexandria pulled in, attempting to flag down security. I pulled right next to them, got of the car, opened his car door, and began to beat him. I yelled across the car at Alexandria that I was going to give her the same treatment after I got done with him. I heard faintly from a distance; Will was making a comment about my kids, telling me it wasn't worth it and that I should think about them. Then I saw and heard the hospital security approach us from a distance. I began to move back to my car, and just like that, they pulled off. As I watched them drive away, I was distraught, still drunk, and still very angry. I spent the night at Will's house hurt, and angry. I literally wanted to kill them.

Tony came back home three days later, and the cycle with us continued. Things between my children and I were slowly deteriorating. I and Jessica couldn't even see eye to eye. Jessica was like most teenagers; into boys, wanted me out of her business, and was barely sharing information with me. However, she did talk to Andrea, and my mother, they were her greatest supporters. When Jessica got mad, all the things they had said about me came tumbling out of her mouth. I often wondered what I did to my mother for her to hate me so much. In 2006, I gave my mother custody of Jessica when she was 15 because she didn't want to live with me anymore. I got in a fight with my sister, behind Jessica's exaggerations, the things that she was reporting to my mother.

Jessica had been telling my mom that all she did was babysit, and she had no free time, leaving out that I paid her good to babysit on the weekends while I worked. I stopped chasing men, hanging in the streets, and I worked so my kids could have the best; that's all that mattered to me at that moment. I was having serious issues with Monica; her problems at school, and her sneaking boys into the house to have sex. When Monica was 16, the school informed me that she had missed a lot of days at school and that her so-called dad was calling her off. I knew it wasn't Jeff since he had stopped seeing his daughter. However, Jeff did step up to help after I had sent our daughter to a detention home. She had become completely unmanageable. I didn't know what to do anymore and my life seemed to be crumbling. The same things I went through growing up seemed to be repeating itself in my children, like a generational curse.

Jessica eventually came back home with me. She graduated from high school, got her first job and first apartment at 19.

Moved in with her boyfriend and we very rarely heard from her. By this time, I had forgotten my suspicions about Tony and Monica, until one day when I had planned to go to the store and I took Monica with me, then Tony objected. True enough, none of my girls really liked him and didn't really deal with him, but this one struck me as odd. I yelled upstairs to my daughters, who were practically in their room and nowhere near him, so why did it matter who went with me?

I thought about what Desmond and Jonathan told me a few days before, about Tony watching porn online, and I didn't know what to think. Him watching it in the daytime, risking the children seeing it. I remember driving one morning and I felt the Holy Spirit so strong on me that I could barely stand up. I had this deep need within me to write. As I was driving the same streets I always did, I noticed things looked wider, bigger and clearer, almost in HD. This was a couple of days before Easter 2010. God had given me a vision; a vision of me in a cold dark basement, with many things piled upon me. I felt extreme peace and no fear, but something was heavy within me. I knew exactly what this was; they were my issues. He had come to rescue me and was here to rescue me. I spent most of my day in prayer and trying to put in words what God had given me. I sat at the table with the Word of God open to Ezekiel and the valley of dry bones, **Ezekiel 37:1.** I started reading aloud, and God began to give me a vision of Tony in the bedroom sitting at the computer looking at things, fantasizing about my daughter. I immediately yelled out to Tony, and as if he could see what I just saw, he just politely walked out the door and never came back. Before I went to sleep that night, I tried to write a letter to my mom, telling her how much pain she had caused me. I often wondered why she didn't love me, and I expressed it to her as best I could. No matter how many times I tried, I couldn't print the letter out on my computer. I finally realized that God was telling me *Not To.* I woke up the morning after Easter to God addressing me as *prophet*. He reminded me of the great story of Anna, the Prophetess, who stayed in the temple after her husband died and worshipped day and night. She also announced the coming of Jesus Christ. I didn't understand the significance but remembered something someone once told me recently. Melissa was her name, an older woman whom I was spiritually connected to, and she called me Anna. God told me that a prophet's hands were always clean and how to prepare myself. I felt I was preparing to go somewhere, but I had no idea where to. I was walking out my door and I heard a man yelling and proclaiming the gospel of Jesus Christ, and he offered me a Bible tract. Besides, Sis. Minnie, I didn't know anyone else at the time and couldn't tell anyone what I was going through (besides my mom), so I headed her way thinking she could help me. I felt she could understand because she was a Christian too. When I got to my mom's house, He began speaking to me about getting up walking, so that is what I did. I got up and started walking, and I could walk fine, and holding on to the wall for added security. God didn't want me holding on to the wall, He wanted me to trust Him. I walked and fell many times, but I got back up and kept on trying. By this time, my mother was pulling up, and I met her at the door and greeted her. I walked in after her, and as she was sitting, I said that I need to pray with her! Just then her house phone rang, and I went to answer it. It was Monica telling me that my friend Kim needed to talk to me. Kim was definitely mad about something since she was on the phone yelling and cussing at me. I said *I rebuke you satan in the name of Jesus* because I knew very well the source, especially at a time like this. I hung up the phone and turned my attention to my mother, who was staring at me. I expected her to be ready to jump into prayer, but as I sat down and looked at her, her face had changed. She immediately told me she did not want to pray, and as she said that an object seemed to have been projecting out of her cheek. With this new vision I began seeing things on top of people's faces and a certain distortion. What I had seen on my mom's face appeared to jump out. I had seen it on Tony's face, and he appeared to be sleeping. Before I got to my mom's house, I was riding down the street and I got to see my little cousin in the car, we pulled over at the gas station to talk and I could barely recognize her, her face had a distortion to it. I was in the Spirit really. I didn't understand right then but I told my mom, that I was leaving and that I was shaking the dust off my feet.

Matthew 10:14, *"And in whatsoever place ye shall enter, and they receive you not, in My name ye shall leave a cursing instead of a blessing by casting off the dust of your feet against them, as a testimony, and cleansing your feet by the wayside"*

I never heard that scripture before that day, but I spoke it, and as I laid in bed that night, I had strange visions about my mother and my sister. God began to speak concerning them, saying my mother was evil and practiced witchcraft. I was totally shocked, "not my mom." The Christian who never smoked or cussed, but He said it, so I knew it was so.

Tuesday came, and I was still full of the Holy Spirit, and still seeing, the Lord even told me that I was going to birth that day. I reached out to Ms. Minnie; this was probably the last time we talked before I saw her that last time. I needed her advice, and direction on this matter. The only advice that she could give me was for me to learn how to breathe, and she said it coldly. Keeping her words in mind I found myself at church that night for an Intercessory prayer. I sat in the front pew, crying out to God until I felt a release in my spirit. When I looked around, I saw a young woman who appeared to be praising God, but God told me she was not. As she walked past me after service, I reached out to hug and speak to her, but she shunned me. Then she gave me a half hug, and when she leaned back, I saw on her face the same look as the one I had encountered at my mother's house. After I got home, we all piled in the car and headed to McDonald's. Even though I didn't have any money, still I heard God tell me to go. When I walked in the door, there was hardly anyone there, but I was greeted by the manager who called me *Prophetess.* I ordered our food and slid every card I had, but none of them had money. The cashier went in the back, got the manager who came up without question, slid a card and paid for our food. The same person who called me *Prophetess;* to me, that was a miracle.

A few days later while sitting at home talking to my M.S. nurse, my girl Diana walked in. She started telling me how Monica and Desiree' had come to her house saying I wasn't well, that I cut my phone off for Jesus and that I wasn't acting right. I assured my girl I was cool, and nothing was wrong. My phone got cut off because I didn't have the money to pay for it. Not only could I see, but I could also hear everything the radio was playing. I could hear voices, could hear laughing and talking, and even as they turned the stations, I could still hear it. I didn't tell anybody, but I seriously wondered if I had lost it mentally at that point, and Because I had just gotten the IV steroids for three days about a week prior. My mother whom I had not spoken to since the day I left, kept trying to convince me that I needed to go to the hospital, because I was not well. They took me to St. Thomas Hospital where I was born and dropped me off saying that they couldn't stay since they needed to run to Uniontown to go see my grandmother, my mom's mom. My grandmother Jesse whom I had not seen since I was a little girl, needed to be seen right then, and they had no car neither of them. I got seen and was on my way out the door after being given a clean bill of health and I called my mom and sister to pick me up. They couldn't find anything wrong with me, but my hospital visit was weird, it was almost like they tried to find something wrong but just couldn't. I called my sister and mom, and they said they just got to Uniontown and that I should just sit tight. Andrea said they would be there soon, but I didn't want to wait, so I called my cousin to pick me up. I got home and fell asleep, only to awake later to the sound of my sister's voice asking the kids if they ate, and if they were okay. After realizing I was up, she told Desiree' to help me to the car, so I could take them home. When I got to the car, my mom was in the passenger seat and Andrea in the driver's seat. I expected Andrea to get out because I had to drop them off, but I noticed on the driver's side door, there was a symbol that had been written on the window that appeared to be a cancer symbol. I told Andrea that I was driving, but in an angry demon voice, she told me that I'm not well. I told her I was and showed her my paperwork from the hospital. I perceived they had done black magic on my car, and what was going to happen when I got in the back seat was nothing nice, but it was serious. My mother was on a walker and because I told her I was driving, they both got out of the car and started walking. *Andrea wasn't getting in the back seat*; the Lord kept speaking *they were going to literally "Drive me crazy."* I backed up my car, parked it, and went in the house. Andrea came by about 20 minutes later and asked to use the phone. The kids handed her the phone through the door, and I continued to lay in bed. Later that night, I woke to my daughter Monica cooking me breakfast, but it didn't smell right. She was cooking bacon, but it smelled funny and was making me sick and paranoid. I didn't know whom to trust anymore, and even my children did not look right in the face. Tony came by briefly to *check on me* and his face and even he didn't look normal. Even though he was walking, he looked asleep. I couldn't take it. I hopped in my car and just started driving.

I ended up at a nursing home in Cleveland, Ohio, and I stumbled up to the door and told them I needed help; I could not even remember my name! From there, I was shipped to an area hospital that had a mental health facility. All this stuff, and all these things I saw, I did not understand, but God was with me. I found out the next day, my cousin Christian took the boys to my sister's house, and Jessica refused to take them. She had to work, I think was her excuse, and my boys ended up at my sister's house. They had not even been there 24-hours before my sister called the cops, telling them she couldn't keep them. There was really no excuse because she had four children and no car. I was there Wednesday, Thursday, Friday, and they let me out on Saturday. When everything became clear, my only concern was my children. Yes, they were in the custody of C.S.B., but there was nothing I could do about it. The hospital was crazy but being there in that short time confirmed in my spirit, that I wasn't crazy. Half of the people who were there weren't crazy either. They just had spiritual conditions, most of them. I wasn't diagnosed with anything, but they called what I had a psychotic episode. The hospital did a lab screen, and not only did I have marijuana in my system but LSD, as well something I never used.

On Friday when I met with the doctor, he said that he didn't see a reason to keep me and that the drugs were out of my system. Never in my life have I ever been diagnosed with anything, except as a child when they tried to stick me with the Bi-Polar diagnosis at 12. So, to hear the doctor say that my sister reported that I was Schizophrenic and that they should keep me, was disturbing. I had been in counseling for stress management for 3 years, never diagnosed with anything, never prescribed any medication, and my counselor saw me regularly, and had no concerns. Please understand this lady [my counselor] had to vouch for me because I really don't think they would have let me leave if she had not, concerning what my sister called and spoke.

I didn't get a diagnosis from them either. When I got in my car and drove back to Akron, back to my life, I knew in my heart I was never dealing with Andrea or my mom. I knew the truth, and I could never ever unsee or unknow all that I heard and had seen. I left that hospital with my soul wounded, and I would never be the same.

Act 26:17-18...

"*[choosing you for Myself and] rescuing you from the Jewish people and from the Gentiles, to who I am sending you to. To open their spiritual eyes, so they might turn from darkness to light, and from the power of satan to God, that they may receive forgiveness, and release from their sins and an INHERITENCE among those that have been sanctified [set apart, made holy] by faith in Me.*"[AMP]

Chapter 14
"Here & Now"

As I drove down the highway coming from Cleveland that Saturday morning, I cried and prayed to God the whole way home. I was still in shock but thankful to God, even though I didn't understand why I had to go through all that. Why did God allow my mom and my sister attempt to kill and destroy me? I wasn't afraid though, since God told me that never again would they ever be able to do that; but I wasn't a fool. God showed me the real deal about them both, so never will I hang around or be vulnerable again near them. The black magic they had done on me obviously didn't work! I arrived home, turned the key, and half of what I owned was gone. I sat there for a little while, then gathered what little I needed and left.

I went to the only place I felt was safe enough, in order to allow myself to process. That was my Grandma Ann's house. I would need time to process but more importantly I would need time to heal, because my soul was wounded. I never want to experience this situation again, and I did not want to see anymore, it was too much. I felt like Moses, when he cried out to the Lord saying he couldn't do what God had asked of him and turned his back on all he knew and never looked back. I briefed my grandma and Aunt Renee about the situation over the phone and asked grandma if I could stay at her house. It wasn't long before I reached her house and when I walked in, I saw my grandmother sitting at the table. It brought me comfort.

She was always reading or had a book in her hand or lying across her bed. I felt safe in her house. I also had a headful of memories, with my dad, grandma, cousins and a boy I used to like and see from the neighborhood just from walking in her house. As I sat down and looked into my grandmother's eyes, I couldn't help but cry. I was overwhelmed in my heart. I was hurt, and above all I still didn't understand why God would let me see and be hurt like that. I set in my mind to *never see* again, and I prayed for it to stop. I was even confused about this *prophet business,* whom I really was, and what in the world God did require of me. I made up in my mind from that day moving forward that I was not cut out for it.

Immediately I assessed my losses; my home, and half of my stuff, my mom, my sister, everything I had was gone except my children who were the most important people to me. I started telling my grandmother and aunt all the events that had occurred within the past few days. As they listened to the story, my aunt re-minded me that was the same scenario that happened to her brother, my dad. I silently thanked God again that He allowed me to survive with my mind intact and able to tell the story. My dad didn't make it and I was sad that he didn't make it, but I did. These were the thoughts swimming in my head as I laid comfort-ably on my grandmother's couch.

I thought about where my life was headed, and I knew I had to get a hold of C.S.B. to see about my children; another battle I had to fight. I had set up to meet with the social worker on Tuesday at my grandmother's house and when I finally got to talk to Jessica, she talked to me like this was a normal occurrence. This wasn't the first time Jessica had turned her back on me; in 2006 I went to jail for domestic violence. I had just got off work and headed home to find that my children were not there. Jessica had been on the phone all day while I was at work talking to my mom and sister about having to babysit her siblings. I paid Jessica to watch them for the days that I worked, and she was 14 at the time. It still didn't stop her from trying to stir up discord. I mean let's just be honest, they didn't like me, and any negativity added fuel to our already burning fire.

I called my sister that night to inquire why my kids were at her house and she got smart with me. When I arrived at my sister's house I was let in and told by my sister and her boyfriend that Jessica wasn't going anywhere. After I asked her to get up and gather her siblings so we could go, Jessica did not move, or budge and I took that as straight disrespect. I snatched her little ponytail, signaling for her to come on. Andrea's boyfriend put his hands on me, trying to stop me from touching Jessica, and in turn I put my hands-on Andrea and guess who was sitting right there during all the drama, my mom. I went to jail for domestic violence, my kids went to C.S.B., and I blamed Jessica, my mom and my sister. Then my mom came up with a better plan, she asked me for custody of Jessica, claiming she could provide a better life for her. My mom provided a house and all the things Jessica wanted, but she still wasn't happy. Her behavior and smart mouth didn't change either. It wasn't long after she was at my mother's house that she complained about my mother, and eventually, my mom started complaining to me about Jessica. Even though I had my personal issues, I loved each one of them and worked hard to provide, for them to have what I felt they deserved even if it came at a big price. I needed all my children to help me because literally we were *all we had* me and my babies. Even though my heart was filled with so much pain and disappointment, I couldn't let my children down. So, it was decided that Jessica would go to her dad's house. Jason, he tried too, and it didn't work either. At 17-years-old she moved back home with me, graduated from high school, and eventually moved out at 19.

As I told my grandma and aunt what I had been through, we all placed my mother at the head of the situation and related it to what happened to my dad. After I spent the night at my grandma's house that first night, God directed me to clean my car of the witchcraft they had put on my car. I spent hours in my grandma's driveway wiping windows down with ammonia to even sweeping the floors, and that's when I found it. It was hidden in the backseat and under the floor mat, a piece of paper, drenched in oil, with words on it. Not telling what would have happened if I would have sat in that backseat, thank God for His mercy. Then Andrea calls up to the hospital and says that I was schizophrenic which I never was. My father was diagnosed with that as a result of the Vietnam War, so they said. True enough when I was younger, I would see him physically act out, but it was not always like that. He was a professional, worked good jobs, had degrees and was very intelligent. It was again mentioned how my mother fed my dad a sandwich and he was never right anymore, according to my aunt Renee. So, we figured that my mom sent those spirits to attack my dad, and she sent them to me too, but God didn't allow it. He let me see the plot and plan and I can thank God wholeheartedly for allowing me to see, but He never told me why. After that, I started my run-away from the Lord, and what He had designed for my life. I made it up in my mind that there is no possible way I could do it, and I asked God if He could get someone else for the job. Some time went by, even months and everything finally did come together. I got my kids back, in June; I got a new place after about three weeks of staying with my grandma and aunt. I walked out of there with a microwave, a washer and dryer, a few outfits and my desktop computer. I wanted to start over and forget all the past behind and that would include Tony because he wouldn't talk to me, wouldn't come see his son and totally abandoned us. He was convinced I was a crazy person after all that my mother had filled his head up with. He wouldn't come around and he wouldn't come see his son. I found out that Tony and Alexandria were back together, and he wasn't allowed to talk to me. The new rule was I had to go through Alexandria about our son. So, she decided to try and befriend me, but knowing her intentions, still dealing with her was hard. Jonathan loved his dad and had never been without him but all she could think about was me getting next to Tony, even though I had my doubts when it came to him and my daughter. However, I was still hurt that he went back to Alexandria because she was clearly controlling him with her money, and this woman hated me so much she called and told me to kill myself as I was in the way of her relationship.

I saw Tony walking one day and I asked him if he needed a ride. When he got in the car, I noticed that he was actually scared of me. Based on what God had revealed to me about him, it was easier for him to believe I was crazy. It didn't take long after that for me to realize that my mom tried to shut me up, but I wonder how long it would take my mother to figure out that it was God's voice speaking and not mine.

Months after my life was coming together, I met a man. I wasn't looking for one though, but this man was attractive, dark complexioned, short, and I was in the car with my boys and my Aunt Sharon at the time. We had just come from shopping at the goodwill, but it was like we clicked instantly. He got in the car with us, and after dropping off my aunt I brought him home with me. He said he had to work soon, and he worked by my house. He introduced himself as Conner and we proceeded back to my room where we could smoke, and talk, and get to know each other. The talk between me and Conner was like we had been old friends that had not seen each other in a while and were playing catch up. I learned that Conner was adopted and never knew his real mother or father and that he grew up in C.S.B. just like me and had been in various foster homes, also like me. He had five kids, all by different women, worked at a restaurant around the corner from my house, and his birthday was 11 days after mine. In my mind he was my soul mate because we had so much in common. I dropped him off at work, and never heard or saw him again, until about two or three weeks later after that initial day. Conner called me out of the blue to apologize for not reaching out sooner, saying that one of my daughters had come on to him and *he felt uncomfortable*. I reassured him he must have misread that, and that would never happen again. I never said anything to the girls because not only did I not believe him, but I also didn't want to believe him. I picked him up that night and our relationship began. Eventually he moved in without asking me; in one day all his stuff was there.

A year after meeting Conner I was having my 6th baby, Jordan born on January 19th which was my mother's birthday. This was it; I wasn't having any more children and I decided to get my tubes tied. I was 37 years old, and I had three girls and three boys, but seven children in total. The seventh one being the one I lost, but I really couldn't do anymore. My pregnancy was easy; I got pregnant in April but didn't find out until June, after I had already dismissed Conner. I ended up finding out with my cousin Jazz after I had been throwing up a week. We took a trip to Planned Parenthood, and after I took the test, I and my cousin sat back in that office waiting for the results that would announce my 9-week pregnancy.

I had already put his dad out in late April early May, after many lies and a whole lot of finding out who Conner really was (aka Beaz). After getting to know him in just a few short months, I agreed with his foster mother's nickname of him being "too much." Beaz proved to be someone that I should have never met from the weird conversations, to his crazy reasonings and thinking's. I felt uncomfortable, because everything centered around him being in control, but I was pregnant before I noticed all this. As it turned out, Beaz and Desiree' my youngest daughter had

gotten close, and I could tell she looked up to him as a father figure as she was only 13. I was having issues with Desiree' and boys,
drinking and drugs, when they all got out of the foster home. Desiree' pulled me to the side and told me that she was sexually active, I blamed Monica for this. I asked Desiree' how she felt and
whether she would do it again, just to see her reaction and where
her head was at. She told me she didn't want to do it again, as she
looked me straight in my eyes. However, over the next several
months, I caught her a few times having sex in my house with
boys. Monica was 16 and decided she wanted to go to Job Corps
and I felt that was a great idea, considering all that we had been
through and what she put herself through.

Both of my girls needed a father, and I felt they both acted out,
because they needed a father's guidance. I had been seeing Beaz a
month and Desiree' was calling Beaz dad and that really bothered
me. I noticed she made it her business to desire to ride in the car
with him. Whenever he went somewhere and I stayed quiet, he
made everything look so innocent. Sometimes when I and Beaz
would talk, he would tell me about his past, and I could tell he
was not ashamed of what he would say. I started thinking he was
weird, that he had a small hatred for God burning in him for all
that he had been through in his past. When I talked about God, he
didn't want to hear it. His idea of family had been tainted as a little child. He spoke regularly about his abuse sexually and physically being in many foster homes much like mine, and that is
what attracted me to him originally.

The whole picture between him and Desiree' started to look
tainted after I had received my Social Security benefits rolling in.
Beaz convinced me to buy an additional car, and of course it was
for him to drive all the time. Desiree' made it her business to tell
him my personal business, and when he would get mad, he would
tell it. Then there was the final straw, Desiree' was on Beaz's
phone screensaver; not all my kids but just her. I told my aunt Re-

nee and my cousin Al to put him out of my house. That was it, or so I thought. The following month, I found out that I got pregnant by this fool. I had planned to have an abortion. Planned Parenthood told me I was past the six-week mark and couldn't take the morning after/abortion pill.

Desiree' started telling people that Beaz raped her and would go to her room at night, but she never told me that, so I didn't find any truth to it. I never did get that abortion the following week and I had an appointment set up for Friday. I never had an abortion and was scared to go through with it. It just so happened some money I was expecting never came by and I remember praying to God asking Him to help me. I could hardly walk; I was on disability, and I was trying to have a baby. I was scared, and as the months went by, I talked to Beaz on the phone, and he promised me he would stick by me and his child. By October of 2011, I decided to move from the house on Bertha to a house up the street on Clifford, basically the same neighborhood. The house on Bertha had a slanted slope, I had to put the emergency brake on when I parked. In the winter of 2010, I had to call a tow truck a few times to pull my car out of the graveled driveway when it snowed, and I wasn't going through that the following winter so in October of 2011, I planned to move and when I did, Beaz helped out and he moved back in with us, convincing me I needed him during this time. I believed him.

Isaiah 46:10, *"Declaring the end and the result from the beginning, and from ancient times the things which have not [yet] been done, Saying, 'My purpose will be established, and I will do all that pleases Me and fulfills My purpose....'"* [AMP]

2 Kings 6: 17-20...

"And Elisha prayed, "Open his eyes, Lord, so that he may see". Then the Lord opened the servant's eyes, and he looked and saw

the hills full of horses and chariots of fire all around Elisha. As the enemy came down toward him, Elisha prayed to the Lord, "Strike this army with blindness", so He struck them with blindness as Elisha asked. Elisha told them, "This is not the road, and this is not the city, follow me, and I will lead you to the man you are looking for" and

he led them to Samaria. After they entered the city, Elisha said, "Lord, open the eyes of these men so they can see". Then the Lord opened their eyes and they looked, and there they were, inside Samaria." [NIV]

Pray this prayer along with me:

Heavenly Father ... open my eyes so that I may see! I can't fight battles if I cannot see, may the Holy Spirit give great revelation and comfort through this journey, allow me to clearly see my purpose, and Your vision for my life. You promised in Your Word You would give us rest from pain and hurt; I release it to You now...

... in Jesus mighty name, Amen.

Chapter 15
"The Saga Continues"

Too much repeat of a thing becomes a pattern but holding it in high regard makes it an obsession that potentially can turn into and addiction. So, when your life seems to repeat the same things, people, places and situations over and over, it becomes insanity. I didn't know what I was doing, why I let him get back in my life, and even more importantly my children's lives. Beaz assured me the past was the past and what I thought was never meant. When we moved to this other house Desiree' constantly ran away and most days she never even came home from school. Desiree' preferred hanging out with her friend's versus being at home, and I never thought for once it could be about Beaz. Beaz treated me badly during the last half of my pregnancy; called me crippled and would take my car for hours. Never gave me any money towards my bills but would get mad anytime I took off in my van. He thought I was his property and I had to get approval just to leave the house. My friends hated him, my boys didn't like him, and he never really paid attention to them. However, Desiree' was his *Rosie*, and she would still jump in and out of the car with Beaz. I had a lot of talks with her about staying out of his face, and to stop asking him for cigarettes. Desiree' even told me that he *was her dad*. I was shocked, but I let it go.

I never let it go actually. In fact, I was paranoid because of what Tony was suspected to have done with my daughter. I snuck up on them quite a bit, listening to conversations and just watching but I never saw anything out of the ordinary. I left my phone a couple times at the house and on record mode to catch some solid evidence and of course I found it. I made up places to go just so I could catch them, and I would rush back home and grab my phone. One day I ran to the corner store, but I was gone for only 25 minutes. When I got back, she was already in the room, and he was in our bedroom downstairs. I took my phone from the re-cliner in my bedroom and went into the bathroom to listen. As I played the recording, the first thing I heard though the first few minutes were silent was Tony calling my daughter's name. I could hear him asking her to massage his feet and I heard her replying yes. I had a problem with that because I was pregnant at the time, and she never once offered to rub my feet. I played Desiree' and told her I heard the whole conversation. I told her that I was shocked at what I heard and that made her tell the truth; practi-cally everything, from how he told her how pretty she was to how much he loved her. I didn't realize, but he was grooming her for something. I got a denial again out of both of them though, but Beaz couldn't keep lying anyway.

I was almost due for my delivery. I often went to my doctor's appointment because I was in my final trimester and close to the 38-week mark. I had to get an ultrasound to see if the baby was in the right position for delivery. When the ultrasound tech detected that my amniotic fluid was low, I was immediately moved to labor and delivery so they could induce me. I was not ready, but I was anxious, because it was the end of my pregnancy and I just wanted it to be over. I wanted Desiree' with me, so she could see the birth, and she could serve as support to me. Even though I was being induced, my active labor didn't start for hours. When the hard pains did start, I clung to Desiree,' and about three that morning, my water broke.

I got an epidural because the pain was so intense, and only after pushing one good time, Jordan made it into this world at 3:41 am. They never had to spank him to cry, he came out screaming. He was 8 pounds, 6 ounces and 21 inches long. Jordan peeked at me when I held him, but he never opened his eyes. Beaz was so excited, I guess he became sober. He came to the hospital drunk, but still he did cut the cord. Beaz left me and Desiree' after the birth and we both tried to crash, but with the nurses in and out I barely slept through the night, excited about my new baby too. Desiree' was fun to have at the hospital. I ordered two trays every time so she could eat with me.

Desiree' and Monica were up here fighting for the baby and trying to get him to open his eyes. When I woke up, we even had a real heart to heart conversation concerning her not wanting to have children and I laughed eventually. After having six kids, I sang that song many times. My girl Mona came to see me and brought me some flowers and candy and showed loved to her nephew. Mona wheeled me downstairs, the hospital didn't let you walk. You had to be pushed via wheelchair.

I quit smoking at seven months of the pregnancy, and I was praying that Jared my baby was negative. I didn't want to give the hospital any reason to suspect I was an unfit mother. Mona pushed me back and we said our goodbyes. Beaz had taken Desiree' to my aunt's house because somehow the nurse found out she wasn't 18. I later found out he actually told them that, so I decided to call and check on her although to my surprise she didn't answer. I came to find out she was going to stay home, complete homework and help Beaz get my room together for the baby. I got instantly angry and hung up to call him next. He didn't answer the first two times but when I finally got him on the phone, Beaz purposely withheld the fact that he never dropped my daughter off. When I confronted him, he had the nerve to get mad at me. I demanded to speak to Desiree' now but Beaz said she was in the shower. I told him to knock on the door and get her. He did, and

I explained to her saying, "you can't stay there." After she passed the phone back to him, I went off, "I don't know what you trying to pull, but she isn't staying with you." He had the nerve to try and say the weather was bad, so I replied to him, "then drop her off, or I'm going to have somebody pick her up ASAP because she will never stay with you." I hung up on him and told my aunt to be expecting her soon. I was angry Beaz tried to pull a fast one on me. Beaz must have forgot the story he told me about his last baby momma and her 17-year-old sister, and he had the nerve to be proud of it. He claimed during his last sons' birth that his child's mother's sister who was 17 and a virgin came on to him. He bragged, "while his son was being born, he was at his girlfriend's house taking her sister's virginity." I felt he was trying to relive that with my daughter who was almost 14 at the time. I called Beaz several times and not once did he answer. He was mad I had ruined his plans and my aunt said it had been a couple hours before he physically brought her. My aunt said, "They did whatever they needed to do before he dropped her off," and I was horrified at the thought. I determined in my mind that as soon as I could, I was getting away from him. I needed him with the baby, I had no one else to rely on at the time but him. Monica was gone, and Desiree' was unreliable after her many run sways. So, I was definitely going to take advantage of the situation and use it to my advantage. Beaz sickened me, with his sick stories and twisted mind. I couldn't wait to get away from him. I got my tubes tied and Beaz would not sign the birth certificate. He picked me up from the hospital with my gas light on and he just got paid the day I had our son. My house wasn't clean and, in the trash, can. There were all kind of empty cans of beer and swisher packs all over my house. I wanted to cry but I held on strong, trusting God would help me. I felt so inadequate and empty, and with no support. I was prepared to do it. I didn't use the walker in the house because I could walk holding on to the wall, and of course I was especially careful with my baby. I did everything for Jordan by myself, and me and Beaz had a system at night; he slept on the couch and Jordan slept in the bed with me, when he would hear him cry, he would warm up the bottle for me. I stayed in my room with Jordan for most of the day because everything was convenient around me. It was hard when the baby wasn't asleep; I had to tend to my other children, and I was tired when Jordan slept. I tried to sleep, but had to clean, cook and take care of the boys. The boys would help as much as they could. They were 6 and 8, and I taught them how to keep an eye on the baby while I was cooking or trying to nap because of exhaustion. Beaz worked almost daily but never had any money. Child Support was getting majority of the money out of his check for his other children and that was the main reason he didn't sign the birth certificate. Not even because he didn't acknowledge his son, but because he didn't want another child taking from his paycheck, although he had money for beer and weed, and he put the bare minimum in my gas tank and constantly drove my car to work and wherever he wanted to go. Beaz hit me a couple times too and seemed to think it was cool to control me. I could not even trust him with Jordan. Twice I came back after he had watched Jordan, and Jordan had a swollen lip; I think something was wrong with him. Jordan didn't like being around him and screamed when he was with him. I finally got the courage to put Beaz out of my house when Jordan was 4 months old. I couldn't do it anymore and I was miserable, and my kids were too, but this was far from any easy task because he didn't want to go anywhere. I called the police right before he got off work. I called them and told them the situation and why I wanted him out of my house. I informed the police that he would arrive in 20 minutes. They said that they would get there in 30 minutes time. Beaz came home like everything was normal. I was sitting on the couch and shortly after he got in and settled down did the knock on the door from the police came.

I told Beaz boldly in front of the police that he had to go, and they made him pack all his stuff and leave by escort. He felt betrayed and to my disgust looked hurt about the situation, but I could care less. Love definitely did not live here anymore. About a month later he started blowing my phone up, talking about how much he missed his son, and kept apologizing to me. I started taking Jordan to see him from time. He was staying here and there, and constantly making it seem as if I was the cause of every bad thing that was going wrong in his life. Beaz didn't get along with anybody; not his baby mama's, not his so-called family, not his coworkers and he didn't have friends at all. I felt sorry for him and would sometimes pick him up to spend the night at my house since it was closer to his workplace. On one of those visits, Desiree' told a friend of hers that Beaz came up in her room in the middle of the night and raped her while she was sleep. Now I didn't hear about this the night it supposedly happened, but the following day. Honestly, I didn't believe her. Beaz was quiet about the whole thing and Desiree' kept telling everyone she could including Juvenile court, at her arrest for running away. I had "them people" in my life again questioning what really happened, but I couldn't provide any details. Besides, I didn't hear any screaming or tussling in the middle of the night. Desiree' and Beaz did not like each other anymore, and he constantly told on her when he got a chance to. He complained about her constantly begging for cigarettes and to hit the blunt, he even nicknamed her Felecia for always begging all the time. I didn't know what to think, or who to believe. I just knew if he did rape her, she would definitely scream. Wouldn't she? And again, her behavior towards him was still the same. I did tell Desiree' not to tell them that story if it wasn't true and she finally told CSB that. They eventually let it go but got really involved with her because of her behavior; her running away and not going to school. The case plan was just for her, but I got a white caseworker who was nosy and doing too much in my personal business and before long they were worried about me. I ended up reaching out to Desiree's grandma in Texas, asking for some help with Desiree'. Her dad and family down there scraped up the money and sent Desiree' a plane ticket. They got her out of Akron, which I thought was best.

As months past I learned to let Beaz go. He moved on with his life and I moved on with mine. It was a struggle because he wasn't trying to let me go, mostly for a solid place to stay. He was definitely seeing somebody else, because when he pulled up at my house, he was driving a nice, newer car, and he never had a license and therefore no stable car. The thought of me messing with someone bothered him because he constantly threatened me and talked about it. I wasn't really dating but I had friends. I had run into an old flame recently, Vic, somebody I had met back in my Rosemary days. Vic's sister Katrina met me at the gas station by my house. She asked me whether I could put her car in my name. She met Jordan during this time, and she fell instantly in love with him, and she started keeping him sometimes, to give me a break. Several times, she kept him overnight. People were willing to help me once I got Beaz out of my life since nobody wanted to deal with him. Katrina and I got close, and she asked me whether she could be Jordan's godmother; I agreed to that. Katrina was my girl despite the things I didn't like about her. She drank, almost always to passing out, but she took good care of her kids, had a nice home and she worked. She just had another side to her that was loud, ignorant and just drunk. One night, I went to pick up Jordan and when I pulled in her driveway, standing outside the porch was her brother and he was drunk. Vic yelled to me, "Hey Dee." I hadn't seen him in years, probably since 2007 when he was working at Dave's Supermarket, rolling them carts. Vic followed me around the store that day, trying to talk to me and to get my attention. We talked briefly before I left the parking lot. Vic was a part of my past which I wasn't into anymore. I had grown up from that "hood girl" who lived in the Rosemary's. I was older and wiser. The first time I met Vic was in 1999, a friend that I recently met from the hood, Tyrone had stopped by and brought him. Tyrone and I were cool then and we never looked at each other in that way, but his friend Vic definitely had something in mind. The day Vic first met me, he kept staring at me ever since he walked through the door. He never said two words throughout the visit. Vic *was fine*, dark skinned, short 5'7, a goatee, short hair, cute haircut, and he dressed nice, but he was obviously a drunkard. Just because a man is fine doesn't mean a woman has to rush to attach to him. I was attractive myself and I definitely was about my business. I was curious about him and what was behind that attractive smile, but I was cautious and wanted to know more about him before I proceeded. They both left and nobody got the number, but I had faith in the fact that the way Vic looked at me, that I would see him again. The way he looked at me and the way our eyes locked on. I guess he also lived around there in the hood. Just like I thought, he showed up to my house with a blunt and the question, "do you want to smoke?" His first question was, "you seen Tyrone?" I let him in. He sat on the couch next to me, and while we passed the blunt between us, he started a conversation. Vic told me I was pretty and dark, and he had to have me. I didn't know what to say. He was trying to touch me, but I wasn't on it. I didn't know him! I gave him my number and he told me he would see me soon. He kissed my forehead and left. I found out Vic was married and had a young son in the parking lot across the street, and I knew his wife. She was a tall, real light skinned lady, she did hair. When I found out truth, I left him alone. He wasn't honest. One of my girls said he'd messed with her before. Every time I saw him, he had a 40 ounce in his hand, and he seemed just like all the men in the projects; drunk, high, no ambition and living off of women. With Vic standing before me I could tell he was happy to see me, but I stomped his hopes out quickly and told him, "Vic you ain't about nothing." Thinking of him in the past, he was drunk and swaying while I was talking to him in front of his sister's house. I gave him my number and address (because he asked). He said he wanted to come by and see me, and then I pulled off. Vic came by the next day to explain that he lived up the street with his girl and her two kids. Christina, his ex-wife had left town with their son, and moved to Detroit, where her family was. It was a combination of the cheating and drinking, and he was unwilling to change, plus the fact that he complained about his wife going to church. Vic complained to me about it though he believed in God. Vic just felt it didn't need all those dramatics and extra stuff. I contemplated telling him my experience, but I knew in my heart he could not understand, neither would anybody else. It was strictly between I and My Father. I hadn't really had much contact with my mom or sister after the incident in 2010 but I thought of my mother often. I felt compelled to call her from time to time to check on her to see how she was doing. Andrea my sister always had problems with staying in her own place. She lived with my mom and her four kids, and sometimes her girl-friend. My sister had been living a homosexual lifestyle since her last child's father cheated on her with one of her friends and de-cided to announce her pregnancy at my sister's birthday party. My heart truly went out to my sister, because if that same sce-nario happened with me, I was definitely going to jail, period. Thank God, nobody has tried me. The last few times I had visited my mom, 2010 and prior, I noticed her new pictures on the wall. Pictures of her and Andrea, and her kids. The whole house was plastered with these photos of her, and Andrea together, then her kids by themselves. My mom had just two daughters; I and An-drea, but if you walked into my mom's house you couldn't tell. I want y'all to understand that never did I see my mom or sister again. When I would call to try to talk to my mom, Andrea would answer really angrily and hatefully, and pretty much like that. Every phone call she made was never friendly towards me, though eventually she passed the phone to my mom at some point. I remembered the days of my spiritual awakening, and the day I walked out there, and she told me to get in the backseat *to take them home*. I would definitely have to get in the driver's seat to get home! Andrea screamed at the top of her lungs at me, "You're not well!" Thanks to God, I was in my right mind because that incident definitely could have taken me out. Andrea, God revealed to me was also involved with the things my mother was into and they were using what they did to manipulate and take people's money. My situation was never off the table, but it was postponed for when the time came. My mother knew exactly whom I was from the time I was a child but waited for it to manifest before she could react. Even with my recent calls to her I could feel her grab her tools and mess with them while she spoke to me. I wasn't scared but was very cautious, and I prayed before and after the phone. I asked Jesus to cover us with His blood. After the phone calls, I felt sick to my stomach and I noticed whenever I encountered that spirit of witchcraft, my stomach went in knots, and it made me feel sad. I only called because I felt that is how God wanted me to treat my mother, with love. My mom got eventually tired from all the phone calls because she could not physically and spiritually get to me, and I did not confide in her anymore. I gave her no access to my life. Two times she told me to leave her alone and stop calling, at the time I was pregnant with Jordan. I had been calling her house, no answer for a couple of weeks. I started calling around asking other family members including my aunt; my mother's only sister Vivian who worked at a nursing home. I could tell from our conversation that she had been told to withhold information, but she told me she would let her know. A week later my mom called me and said, "Please stop looking around for me." She asked me to basically leave her alone and stop calling her. This was a shock, but believable, and hurting. My mom had been in the hospital for her heart, and I was just concerned. The second time, she said that it was in 2013 when she asked me not to call her, and after that time I never did. My dumb self started messing with Vic again. After that initial day, I saw him regularly though he had girlfriend. Despite this reunion with Vic, I was depressed about Beaz and how he treated me, haunted me, and still hurt me. I started spending a lot of time on social media.

One day I received a message from Roland and when I saw the name, memories began to flow. I was ecstatic about opening this message, excited about the contents. Roland was one of my very early boyfriends and technically my first love. It has been 20 years since I had left Oesterlen, the group home in Springfield, Ohio, after all the havoc I had caused there, and after they ended up sending me back to jail in Akron. I left Roland and didn't even get a phone number or address, so I never heard from him until that moment he wrote to me. As I opened the message it said, "Hi Addie this is Roland, I was wondering where you in a place called Oesterlen back in the day?" I replied yes, Roland, I remember you!!! We exchanged numbers and talked over the phone the next few days and we both tried to fill each other in on what we had been doing over the years. We reminisced on the past as I quickly realized he remembered way more about the past than I did. Roland wanted to thank me for all the kind words and encouragement from back when we were kids and wanted to be there for me in any way he could. He lived 30 minutes from me in Cleveland, Ohio, and he was married and had a daughter by someone else. Roland worked and was good at fixing things, then he started to come down to visit me immediately. He was Mr. fix it, in my life, and around my house. Whatever I needed, whether it was money, help around the house and yard work, he did it with no hesitation, and we weren't dating or sleeping together. Roland loved my sons, and he took time with them to help them develop into young men, and they loved him too. Roland did tell me he deserved to get some sex, but I said no. He was married and now that I had gotten older, I wanted to try to respect God and not deliberately sin. I feared God and wanted to be nowhere near God's wrath for my disobedience. I longed for God in ways that I could never express, and it was deeper than I even knew. When I was with Beaz and I was pregnant, I remembered being so depressed that I prayed and asked God to take me. I no longer had the drive to want to live and just like that my mood changed and picked up, but it was hard to maintain it with consistency. I started reaching again towards God.

Roland had been boxing for years and had been training really well. He started talking to me about making a career out of it, but he couldn't do it in Cleveland. He wanted to go to L.A. I supported his vision and we talked about my coming to his boxing matches, and what I would wear, and how he would send for me and the children. Me, him and the kids spent all day together, shopping at Walmart, going out to eat, next I put the kids in bed. We sat out in the car, smoked and talked, and that's when he shocked me with, "I'm leaving my wife, moving to L.A. to pursue my career in boxing and I need you to support and be there for me." I couldn't believe this! Roland said his wife would not support him because she thought this was a childish dream, but he was serious. I vowed to be there for him, and before we parted, we made a bond and promise to each other. He left me some money, and he left for L.A. I sent him a message on FB about how awesome our night was. High on the thought of true love and the fact that he searched and found me, I felt so special though that quickly ended when I received the return message, "Girl I don't want you. What we had was nothing." He called me ghetto and said his wife was better than me, and he had the nerve to ask, "Why would I want you?" He dogged me out, I felt terrible, but it was what it was, and I had definitely been in worse situations. My hope for love didn't matter anymore. As time went on, as I slowly let Beaz go, I started feeling better about myself. I just didn't know how to get out of this rut.

Over the years I had become ghetto, a promoter of crime and basically when it came to money, I was willing to do almost whatever for my children and to get what they needed. I was a hustler, but more than that I was a schemer. I constantly thought of crafty ways to get money, to survive; from stealing to keeping all my receipts and going back to the restaurants saying I didn't get my food. I had certain receipts from places I went and when money was low, we still could still eat what we wanted. I was so used to getting over it became so easy. I was the queen of manipulation. I stole at least 4,000 worth of items within a few days from stores, things I needed and the others I sold to get money. I had a "savage mentality, 'that I was always in need, I did what I had to do to survive and take care of my children.' I hated men, I was distrustful, disloyal, and carried the notion that what all men were sex and money. I was cautious with everybody including my kids. But then I desired a change finally, after all these years. I was tired of going through the same viscous cycle with men and my life. I was truly tired.

I ended up having to move from the house on Clifford because of eviction. I didn't fill out some paper for Section 8 and ended up losing my subsidy and was unable to pay the $750 AMHA was paying. I even requested a hearing and did fill the paperwork out and they still denied me. By this time, I did hear from Roland again, and found out then it wasn't him who left me that nasty message. It was his ex-wife, though he later apologized for it. After a few months in L.A., things had taken a turn for the worse. He was homeless, sleeping in the car and couldn't find a job. The boxing thing wasn't doing great either, with a record of 17 losses and 8 wins. Roland decided to return to OHIO and take another route. He asked me whether he could stay with me, and whether we could try to be in love once again. Honestly, after everything I felt obligated. His wife divorced him while he was gone and used the message on FB and him moving to LA as abandonment. Those were her legs to stand on, plus she had money and resources, but I had nothing. I wondered why he left such a good life to come deal with me. I was so needy, and I didn't have anything. Roland helped me pack and he moved us to our new house on Chittenden, in the hood on the lower East Side nicknamed "Down the Way." I found a nice house with a fenced yard and a garage, all on one floor, ceramic floors and regular rent. When I went to look at the house, there were a group of teenagers standing in front of it. I had a black landlord, and he was nice, and for 600 it was home. The kids loved the house, the big yard and just the neighborhood. Vic came by one day, while I was cooking, cleaning and taking care of the baby. He offered to take Jonathan and Desmond for a tour around the neighborhood and down to his stomping grounds two streets over, in Joy Park. Roland stayed for a little while and went right back to his ex-wife. I didn't love him, but I loved the fact that he was so in love with me. We did a lot of things together and he bettered my life. He helped with the bills, took care of my car and helped me work my legs and strengthen my body. Even though I wasn't head over heels in love with him, my aunt Renee when she met him said "he is not your type but if he loves you, it will eventually grow on you." At 38, I had never been in love, had 6 kids and I was content on being by myself, even though on the inside I was lonely. I was willing to be loved, but I wasn't opening my heart for anyone. I hadn't messed with Vic since the late summer and it was October, though we were still friends. Vic and I talked about him coming to work and to be my home health aide, and that he did that kind of work and wanted to help me with the boys. Vic said it would take him 2 weeks to get everything together and start. I contacted the agency and got the ball rolling. October 13, 2013, due to constant referrals to CSB from Alexandria, and Tony lying to Jonathan, Tony and Alexandria had plotted and planned to take my son away from me. Because of my disability, they made every excuse on why I couldn't take care of them. Behind my back my social worker and Alexandria became good friends. Apparently, her and the social worker Erin felt the same way. They felt I was incapable in raising my children. No neglect or anything happened but a white, older home health aide that had given a bad report, and I couldn't blame her. She might have been asked a tricky question. This worker who had been to my house twice said she observed Jordan run out the door while she was coming through. I begged her to give a favorable account, "Jordan running out the door when someone opened it, he didn't run in the street or get hurt, was normal for a child of his age. It had happened with other kids of mine, the difference was I couldn't chase him, but I could walk and drive and do everything else." That was all CSB needed. October 13, Erin my caseworker knocked on my door with two police officers by 4 pm evening time. She said coldly, "We have concerns, and the children must be removed today." Erin never gave any details and they had already planned this; to give Jonathan and Desmond to Alexandria for her custody and she was no relation to our family. She put Jordan in a White foster home which I thought was so cruel. He was a baby and only 18 months. Jordan had never been away from me, neither had the boys, who were 7 and 9. Before Erin came, the boys were getting a haircut and my house was clean. However, that still didn't matter to them. I stood there helpless as they took my kids away. I couldn't do nothing, and it was all because of my disability. They quickly told me court, a shelter care hearing was in two days and by law, a judge has to review your case to learn what is in the best interest of the child. This is also where CSB represents their case, and they move forward to a case plan or give the children back. They filed dependency and neglect charges on me. The Magistrate whom we went before knew me well. Monica and Desiree' had frequently been in his courtroom. The magistrate had seen me on my feet before, but for a walker to be pushed in a wheelchair, he knew I was a good mother, and I loved my kids. After he heard from CSB and from me, and my lawyer, he made the decision to award my children back to me immediately. I left there happy I won, and all I had to do was wait at the house for them to bring my kids home. The house was clean and put together as I waited for my children. Two to three hours had passed, and I decided to call Erin. Erin wasn't in the first two times, so on the 3rd call I asked to speak to her supervisor. My heart dropped as I told her whom I was, and she began to say, "Ms. Barnett, the Magistrate did order the kids to come home today, but our lawyers filed a motion to overturn the judge's decision and override it. It was called a Stay. CSB had filed a STAY. It was October 15, 2013, and the next court hearing scheduled was January 31, 2014, past Thanksgiving, Christmas, and all of the boy's birthdays, and I was supposed to be cool with that? I was distraught, and the only one I could turn to was God. I needed Him; this was way too much! The day they took my kids and left, I cried, got in my car and hopped on the expressway as I almost closed my eyes and let go of the steering wheel. I didn't want to live if I didn't have my babies, but that sorrow and pain turned into determination to fight for my kids, because I needed them, and they needed me. I had to fight, and I knew God would help me as I ran to Him. I needed support too, so I visited every church around me to find a church home. I finally settled at The Upper Room on Inman St. up the street from my house, right off of Lovers Lane. I could walk there; it was so close. The pastor was a woman, and she could preach, and the Spirit of the Lord was felt up in there. I had my pastors support and for the church, they were praying for me and were willing to be of any support they needed to be. I felt so loved at church I invited my girl Diana with me. She lived a couple blocks from the church. We went faithfully together, and God revealed we were like Elijah and Elisha. In all these years of being my friend God was rarely something we discussed. She was a sister to me, and we had a lot of secrets between us. God knows how much dirt we did together.

The story of Elijah and Elisha was so interesting, and what did that mean to me. Elijah was a prophet and so was Elisha. After Elijah was taken, Elisha received a double portion of the anointing Elijah had. Elijah indeed was great and did many miracles in his lifetime, but he was tired, and he raised up Elisha to take his place. In addition to the church, I called Roland for support. I seemed to be alone and in need of so much support. I just needed someone. I knew Roland loved me, and I needed to feel that. I had no other support and of course he was there, moved in, got a job and started helping me with the bills. He was loving, attentive, and always there to help me try to get my kids back. He was at every visit supporting me. Vic was there too as my home health aide. He kept my house clean, talked to me, and was a true friend to me. Messing around between us ceased before Roland came back around. I made it real clear to Roland that I would not live-in sin of fornication, so on December 8th of 2013 I married Roland at my church. One of the ladies who put together the wedding told me after, "Addie that man is not your husband." But we had been counseled by the pastor prior to the wedding. They had such a beautiful ceremony and decorated the church so beautifully. My best friend Diana stood next to me as my maid of honor, and we went through all this trouble only for the marriage to last 45 days. Roland cheated on me with his ex-wife, next he got mad at our conversation about my daughter. He told me I should give up on my 16-year-old daughter Desiree' because she was a lost cause. Desiree' had been back from Texas, since her grandma drove her all the way back. She reported Desiree' to be with a pimp and that she was doing drugs. I sent Desiree' to her dad, but during her stay with him, he decided to go on a crack binge and leave his daughter. When she hadn't seen him for years, due to him being in prison, her grandma brought her back. Since Desiree' got back to me, I couldn't take care of her, so I sent her to a foster home, and was now debating if I should let her come home again.

Roland stormed out of nowhere and said he was going to work out at the gym, and this was 6pm. He didn't come back until 1 pm the next day. Vic was there and as I was talking to him, sharing my feelings on this. Roland pulled up and got me worried. He walked in and said nothing. I asked him, "where have you been?" He still didn't answer. I went inside his car for something and on the passenger side there was a long receipt for the Dollar Store with an address of East Cleveland that morning. I quietly went into another room to call his ex-wife in confidence, while he was shut up in another room playing music. She said that he came to her the previous night desiring to have a talk, but one thing led to another unfortunately, so they spent a night of passion together. I was furious and I felt betrayed at the same time. Just like in January right before my court hearing, I went off! His ex-wife knew nothing about me, didn't even know that we got married and she remembered the day we got married that he called her, asking her if there was any chance for them. In fact, he was late to the church on our wedding day, like he had second thoughts. I told Roland that he had to go, and that it was over, and I meant it. Guess who was there as an immediate shoulder to cry on? Vic. In fact, he predicted this whole ordeal. Since I and Vic stopped dealing, he would make comments to me, but he was still with his girlfriend of 10 years and wanted to keep me as a side chick. Not having or seeing him for days got annoying. Since he worked here, I had seen another side to him which I had never seen before, a caring and compassionate person. He took his job seriously and was here promptly and daily. Vic drank a lot, passed out at times,

I was loyal to him nevertheless, and he was there for me.

Once, I had a vision right after I got married to Roland. In this dream/vision, I looked in the rear-view mirror at Vic who was in the backseat of my car and Roland was in front, and I was driving him around looking for jobs; that meant something to me though I can't quite explain.

Vic was my home health aide of course, and it was work hours. I never messed with Vic since Roland left. We weren't flirting or anything. It was strictly a job, although he once tried to. Once, he came in and asked whether he could lay down next to me as I lied on the couch. I told him, "NO and STOP IT." At another time, after my marriage with Roland when I walked to my car, I heard Vic say, "Is it that all it takes is a ring?" I wondered whether he was jealous. I moved on nevertheless, and I wasn't scandalous. I didn't even tell Roland that we used to have a thing because it was over. Vic and Roland were cool, and if Roland knew about Vic's feelings, he definitely would have felt some way.

In my vision I was in my room in my bed, Roland wasn't there but Vic was. Roland was at work. We had the door shut and locked, so I knew we were up to no good. We were about to do something and then all of a sudden Roland was trying to open the door from outside and he began to ask why it was locked. Vic was looking for a hiding spot, and I was trying to get back dressed. Then there was the dream I had a couple days after my wedding. I was at a club or a house party because I remembered walking down some steps and stopping in the middle because someone was there, sitting on the steps. As I attempted to pass him, I recognized whom it was. It was someone I had gone to school with. He said, "Hey girl, question for you. Why would you get married knowing how many men you still have in love with you?" I woke up shocked. God revealed to me even though I had a right intention to get married, my motives were wrong. I didn't marry Roland because I loved him, but because I didn't want to have the guilt of living in sin. I was content, but not happy. I and Roland's divorce was finalized in May of 2014. He paid for it all and got married again to his ex-wife. I never heard from him again, and even when I reached out to him, he blocked me immediately. Roland had a lot of emotional issues that kept me feeling like, I made the right decision in walking away from him, and I never cried once. Pain had made me so strong, as well as all the dirty stuff he said in the end including, "You ain't never going to get your kids back." This provided a solid steppingstone to win. When it came to God, I was relentless; When it came to my children, I was determined. CSB tried their best to ruin my life, but I fought hard! I wrote a letter to the State of OHIO and got Erin off my case for discrimination. Erin made a statement, "I was parenting from a wheelchair" indicating I was incapable of parenting my children because of my disability. CSB lies and used other agencies to lie for them. They used any means necessary to obtain children and most of them for no real reason. Money was the motive behind a lot of these organizations and the enemy was in control of them. Satan had regions and territories, and wickedness in high places. I completed every program, went to counseling as well as everything they said. Alexandria and Tony asked for custody. They had a lawyer and they had money, but they were still denied. As I heard all these lies and things spoken against me, the Lord God spoke, because I felt so alone. "Many more are with you, than with them." I thought about Elisha telling the servant to open his eyes and I look around. On our side in court, it was me, my pastor, lawyer and Vic. On their side, it was about 20 people. I knew the Lord God was with me. They took Erin off the case and gave me a Christian caseworker. Besides, I had favor from the Magistrate. Despite what he heard; he knew the truth. Nothing and nobody could stop it. My kids came home November 6, 2014, and Vic too. He had left his girlfriend of 10 years. Vic stuck by me through everything, and I was so grateful. I was happy for once and I could live again with the man I loved, and everything was going to be just fine. Then, on January 3, 2015, we woke up to find out Vic's only son had slipped into a coma and a few days later died. My mother was found dead by her brother with her face down; dead in her apartment in September of 2015. We couldn't run from pain no matter how much we wanted to be happy. It is inevitable, just like death and it goes on to no end. We can't stop it and we can't even blame God for it. It's a part of our life cycle, and we got to deal with it. I have testified of His goodness and how He brought me through it, and I know He helped me through it. I know now, I never would have made it through it without Him. Carrying me and staying by my side. Never would I have made it! God was always there!

In Conclusion

Isaiah 43:19 (AMP) says:

"Listen carefully, I am about to do a new thing,
now it will spring forth; Will you not be aware of it? I will even put
a road in the wilderness, Rivers in the desert."

This is the season of New Beginnings. I declare this over your
life right now! No longer do we have to live with the guilt of hurt
and pain anymore. The purpose of Jesus' birth death and resur-
rection was to set us free and so we can walk in freedom. The purpose of this book was to expose my pain and release it. All that
I have been through has made me strong in Him because I chose
to lean on Him.

I want to leave you with these kind encouragements for your
soul. God is loving and wants the best for us. It doesn't matter
how many times we mess up; He always welcomes us with loving
arms and remember nothing can separate us from His love! What
can separate us from the love of God? NOTHING! NOBODY!

God's Everlasting Love
Romans 8 NKJV

31 What then shall we say to these things? If God *is* for us, who
can be against us? 32 He who did not spare His own Son, but delivered Him up for us all, how shall He not with Him also freely
give us all things? 33 Who shall bring a charge against God's
elect? *It is* God who justifies. 34 Who *is* he who condemns? *It is*

Christ who died, and furthermore is also risen, who is even at the right hand of God, who also makes intercession for us. 35 Who shall separate us from the love of Christ? *Shall* tribulation, or distress, or persecution, or famine, or nakedness, or peril, or sword? 36 As it is written: "For Your sake we are killed all day long;
We are accounted as sheep for the slaughter." 37 Yet in all these things we are more than conquerors through Him who loved us. 38 For I am persuaded that neither death nor life, nor angels nor principalities nor powers, nor things present nor things to come, 39 nor height nor depth, nor any other created thing, shall be able to separate us from the love of God which is in Christ Jesus our Lord.

If you have accepted Christ Jesus as your personal Lord and Savior, consider yourself an heir of Yahweh, and start viewing yourself a son or a daughter of His!

And whatever God has promised over your life He shall perform! Remember that through your journey!

I love each and every one of you!!
God's many blessings be upon you.

"Father God, I thank you for helping me complete this book. I pray that everything You set out to accomplish through this book and through me and through each and every person that touches this book be accomplished and established. You are God alone and I give You all the glory. Help us turn our pain to you and not allow it to destroy us. I bind the enemy and the strong man of each and every house that is not represented by Christ, restoration, healing and deliverance. I speak over your life! Surrender, receive salvation, conversion and allow the Holy Spirit to move in your life, in Jesus mighty name it is done! Amen"

Addie M. Griffin

Stay tuned for part 2, the sequel The Power of Love.

Here is a preview:

1 Peter 4:8 Amplified Bible (AMP)

Above all, have fervent *and* unfailing love for one another, because love covers a multitude of sins [it overlooks unkindness and unselfishly seeks the best for others].

Chapter 1... In need of desperate change.

I don't think we realize we are so broken and messed up until we get out of the broken situation, begin to heal and our perspectives begin to change. The further we are away from a situation; we begin to see correctly once our blindness begins to clear up and those situations and people who were toxic move farther away from us.

I am a firm believer in 'time heals all wounds,' some deep and hurtful situations take longer, but once you make up your mind to walk away, healing can begin.

As I'm starting this 1st chapter of the Power of Love, I am reminded of some pain I experienced recently. The pain wasn't visible to the naked eye, I still dressed nice, kept my hair done and a smile on my face. I liked to dress nice and smell good and I kept my hair done. I was so used to keeping my appearance up on the outside, and ignoring and masking the pain on the inside, that this was routine.

You didn't even know if we were so called close, because in reality I was never close to anyone, even if we were in a relationship or I called you a friend. The truth was deep down inside, I never trusted anybody and was not close with anybody, of course I went through the motions in life, but besides God, nobody could be trusted. Most people would think that was prideful or I was acting funny, but my reasoning had nothing to do with that, true I was guarded and untrusting, after countless times of being betrayed and my trust abused, when I had genuine intentions. I was tired and at this point every friend, even my children, everybody I knew had either stabbed me in my back, hurt me deeply, misunderstood me, or turned their back on me feelings and deepest thoughts had to be kept inside and hidden from the world. Holding it in had become so damaging, I turned to God often. He may have not always answered, but by faith I knew He was always there, and He heard me. I also learned to just write and allow my feelings to flow on paper.

I learned this powerful truth about Him; constantly being abandoned by people, hurt and betrayed by the people I loved and trusted the most. I still ended up alone, hurt and betrayed, it was in those hurt moments I turned to Him for comfort, and He was always there waiting. In fact, His everlasting love I understood after He rescued me miraculously after I put myself continually in a hurtful situation and He kept warning me and I still didn't listen, and He still had mercy upon me and saved me from one of the hardest trials in my life. The consistent, unchanging LOVE of God finally changed me, it changed me, started making me become whole, it started repairing those broken places in me! The lies I told myself started melting away and I begin to see TRUTH! The Word of God came alive in me, and I began to heal. I realized the Love I had searched for was with me, and within me. I couldn't see it always because of my constant issues, the constant hurt, the distractions, they, weren't sent by God, but they were allowed to make me strong and used to benefit me for my good. Romans 8:28 And we know [with great confidence] that God [who is deeply concerned about us] causes all things to work together [as a plan] for good for those who love God, to those who are called according to His plan *and* purpose. I knew I was His child. I had a purpose and no matter what I had done, He still loved me! And since I was His child, He was consistently there.

The enemy consistently told me I was a horrible person, bad, incapable of change, even had people in my life constantly remind me, of my past faults and I had a lot of them. I became so broken I didn't even desire to be fixed, just to be comfortable. I could take the pain, I just needed comfort from time to time. Drugs, fake friends and men that abused me became my comfort zone, and again I was tricked by pain to ride with him again to more pain. I began a self-hatred of myself for my constant mistakes. My naysayers were my cheerleader section, they knew as long as I was in pain, I couldn't see God's plan for my life. Father would give me dreams and often call me Daughter, but pain had blinded me to the point that I couldn't see. When I saw awesome vision and He spoke awesome things about who I was in Him, I couldn't see it, pain and the enemy blocked it. I asked Yahweh consistently was He sure He called and chose me, because from my view, I definitely didn't see it.

For all your book publishing needs please contact us! Let's make your book dream a reality. Your words hold value, and your readers are waiting.

www.candacejoyner.com
Candacejoyner2020@gmail.com
(910) 416-9988

Made in the USA
Columbia, SC
14 July 2021

41840044R00085